W9-BKW-505

CALVINISM AND THE RELIGIOUS WARS

CALVINISM AND THE RELIGIOUS WARS

BY

FRANKLIN CHARLES PALM

HOWARD FERTIG

NEW YORK · 1971

HOWARD FERTIG, INC. EDITION 1971
Reprinted by arrangement with Holt, Rinehart and Winston, Inc.

Library of Congress Catalog Card Number: 78-80579

PRINTED IN THE UNITED STATES OF AMERICA
BY NOBLE OFFSET PRINTERS, INC.

CONTENTS

Chapter I

CALVIN IN GENEVA

Calvinism has been the object of severe criticism by many sincere men. To them it is a harsh, a narrow, and a hypocritical religion. In their opinion its founder, John Calvin, was sick, incapable of seeing anything but wickedness. Tortured by a variety of painful diseases, he tried to overcome the maladies of his own body, or of the body politic, "by direct effort of will." Refusing to yield to fever and to weakness in himself, he also dealt with the vice and frivolity of others, which he detested, with ruthless application of power, hunting them with spies and breaking them upon the wheel. Many today believe that a "gentler, more understanding method would have accomplished more, even for his own purpose." Yet Calvinism, whether justifiable or not, was one of the most potent factors in the history of France during the larger part of the sixteenth century. It also influenced and sometimes dominated political and economic as well as religious development in the Netherlands, Scotland, and England during the same period and for many generations thereafter, and was carried into the New World to constitute the cornerstone of New England civilization. Even the twentieth century, at first glance so far removed from John Calvin and all his works, is still influenced in many ways and very powerfully by Calvinistic ideas.

CALVIN'S EARLY LIFE

Calvin was born July 10, 1509, in the little town of Noyon in northern France. His father, Gérard Cauvin, was secretary to the bishop of Noyon and fiscal agent for the district. This position enabled the family to occupy an honorable and well-to-do station in society and to mingle with the prominent people of the community. When John was only seventeen an unfortunate incident occurred. His father was accused of financial irregularities, which ultimately led to his excommunication. Today his guilt is still a mooted question.

Calvin's mother was a woman of piety whose influence on her son was slight because she died soon after his birth. After her death Gérard Cauvin was confronted by the difficult problem of supporting and training his six children. Desirous of procuring for Calvin the best education available, he sent him to the home of an aristocratic friend, where through happy association and friendships Calvin developed a certain grace of manner and ease of social bearing which the more humbly trained reformers generally lacked. In 1521, the ambitious father, realizing that John would soon be ready to enter college and that he could not afford to send him, procured for his son a share in the revenues of an ecclesiastical holding. Thus provided with funds, John was able to secure a liberal education, spending four years (1523-1527) at the college of Montaigu, at Paris. Here he studied scholastic theology under the able Noël Béda, and became well acquainted with the Bible, the *Imitation of Christ*, and the works of Augustine. At the university, Calvin won for himself a reputation for marked abilities, for strenuous and critical morality, and for earnestness. His classmates remembered him chiefly because of his fault-finding disposition, and called him "the accusative case."

About the time John was completing his studies in Paris, his father was trying to settle his financial difficulties with the religious authorities at Noyon. This trouble probably explains why Gérard agreed with the anti-ecclesiastical inclinations of his son, and decided to permit the latter to change from theology to law. Leaving Paris, the young Calvin studied at the universities of Orléans and of Bourges, coming under the influence of several heretical professors. Upon the death of his father another important shift occurred in Calvin's life. He gave up the study of law and devoted himself to the classics.

This change was not unusual at that time. France, under the brilliant and ambitious Francis I (1515-1547), was enjoying a "revival of learning" in which the fertilizing influence of classical literature was especially evident. "Everywhere, north of the Alps no less than south, there was a spontaneous efflorescence of intellectual activity." Influenced by this development Francis I had established certain "royal readers," who represented the new humanistic impulse against the conservatism of the Sorbonne. Meanwhile Calvin, young and critical, gladly decided to devote his life to those studies which would enable him to criticize the present and to glorify the past. Perfecting himself in Greek and Hebrew, while studying the classics, he became a humanist, publishing in 1532 his *Commentary* on Seneca's *De Clementia*.

In general the humanists were those Renaissance scholars who, in contrast with most medieval writers, refused to despise or to neglect the pagan works of ancient Greece and of Rome. Claiming that men should enjoy themselves in this world, as did the ancients, they were unwilling to subscribe to the prevailing importance of salvation in guiding the activities of man. They exalted human nature, which they believed to be capable of much improvement, instead of being fundamentally bad. These so-called pagan humanists rebelled against the medieval asceticism which taught that the flesh was an ally of the devil.

Some humanists succeeded in combining the teachings of the pagan writers with the religious doctrines taught by Jesus, Paul, and the church fathers. These new intellectuals continued to believe implicitly in the tenets of New-Testament Christianity, but at the same time they drifted away from medieval asceticism. They were the so-called Christian humanists, who advocated reforms within the Catholic church but refused to break with that institution. Erasmus of Rotterdam and Lefèvre of Paris were especially noteworthy as leaders of this group. Undoubtedly they influenced Calvin to engage in his profound study of the Bible and other religious works.

Calvin refused to remain a Christian humanist. Like Luther, Loyola, and others, he experienced in 1533 a conversion and embarked on a religious career. According to Calvin the summons was definite. A sudden beam or flash of light came from God, "putting him to the proof and showing him in how deep an abyss of error and filth he had been living." He then decided that God had asked him to leave the Roman Catholic church. This he did, and within a year Francis I expelled him from France.

Religious reformers encountered the bitter opposition of the king of France. Francis I had settled in 1516 the religious problem to his satisfaction by arranging a concordat with the pope. This gave him the right to appoint bishops and to dispose of important benefices. Considering himself head of church and state, he opposed any movement which would threaten religious unity and would thus weaken his position. Moreover, Francis I was interested solely in the sensual and artistic sides of the Renaissance, not in the Christian. He and the majority of the French people also felt little desire to break with the Roman Catholic church. Many Frenchmen, however, sincerely believed that this institution needed reforms.

THE ROMAN CATHOLIC CHURCH

In the Middle Ages the Roman Catholic organization was the mightiest institution in western Europe. It controlled the spiritual destiny of every man, woman, and child through the operation of its courts, its sacraments, and the exercise of its enormous temporal as well as its spiritual power. It also surpassed all national governments in wealth, in social prestige, and in actual authority. Shortly after the dissolution of the Roman empire, the church became virtually the sole exponent of peace and the leading center of intellectual activity. Assisting Charlemagne in the building of his empire, preserving precious books—among them the Bible, the works of Aristotle, and the church fathers—and establishing the only schools in western Europe, it richly merited the privileges it enjoyed during the Middle Ages.

Gradually the church became too wealthy. Many nobles and other rich men bequeathed their property to this institution in order to save their souls. Numerous monasteries became centers of vast estates. The head of the church, the pope, governed as a temporal ruler in the Papal States around Rome. This wealth and temporal power only served to arouse the jealousy and the opposition of secular authorities. In the twelfth and thirteenth centuries the pope was strong enough to check the temporal aspirations of his outstanding rival, the Holy Roman emperor.

At the close of the thirteenth century the power of the papacy began to wane. The humiliating Babylonian

Captivity (1309-1377) at Avignon in France (where the head of the church was dominated by the French king); the Great Schism, 1378-1418 (when three popes claimed the papal throne); and the twenty years in which the supremacy of the papacy was contested by church councils, were all evidence of the decline in temporal power of the church, especially that of the pope, and the rise in his place of the powerful monarchs of the early modern period. Moreover, the influence of the pope was restricted to the Christian church in western Europe, because of the existence of the Greek or Orthodox Catholic church in the Balkans and in Russia. This organization refused to recognize the supremacy of the Roman pontiff.

Nevertheless, the pope, at the opening of the sixteenth century, was still a powerful sovereign. He issued decrees which could not be declared null and void by secular rulers. He claimed to be supreme over his clergy and the arbiter by whom all disputes between nations, as well as between individuals, could be settled. Sending ambassadors and legates to various courts, he believed that he had the right to absolve anybody from obedience to laws which he declared unjust. He placed himself above all temporal power, and asserted that he alone was God's representative to all men on earth.

To carry on the work of the Catholic church, taxes had to be collected. Trouble occurred. Financial abuses in ecclesiastical administration bore heavily upon the common people and created serious scandals. Many plain individuals, such as peasants and artisans, begrudged the numerous and burdensome religious taxes, and an increasing number felt that they were not getting the worth of their money. Kings and princes, coveting the great possessions of the church, were only too glad to use this opposition as an excuse for depriving that institution of its wealth.

A crisis was reached when the Christian humanists attacked, in their works, papal power, monastic discipline, and the efficacy of the sacraments. These humanists were assisted in their assaults upon the church by many theological mystics who believed that the institution had become too worldly and that there was in the church too much empty formalism and too little emphasis upon personal piety. The mystics, in particular, strove to warn their pupils against the reliance on what they called "outward deeds," as contrasted with inner faith, feelings, and emotions. Books like the *Imitation of Christ* emphasized the need of love and of faith, rather than of "works." In other words, the mystics tried to weaken the power of the clergy by laying stress on the relation between the individual soul and God, in which relation, they asserted, the sacraments played a very insignificant part.

By the opening of the sixteenth century, many reformers favored the abolition of definite abuses within the church. They claimed that a reformation was much needed. Simony, the sale of ecclesiastical positions, and nepotism, the giving of religious offices to relatives and friends, were condemned. The sale of indulgences, in which alms-giving by a person took the place of doing penance and helped to remove temporal guilt, was especially criticized. In fact, centuries earlier the question had often been raised as to the necessity of so many feast days, pilgrimages, relics, and "good works." A number of men even went so far as to preach the doctrine of the priesthood of all believers and to advocate the abolition or the simplification of many dogmas and ritualistic practices of the church. Bewailing the indolence, ignorance, and immorality of certain monks, priests, and bishops, they prayed for a general reformation. Finally, in 1517,

Martin Luther started the religious revolt in Germany when he developed the doctrine of "justification by faith alone."

CALVIN BREAKS WITH ROME

John Calvin, by his conversion in 1533, not only accepted these ideas, but also left the Roman Catholic church. Because of the growing persecution he gave up the benefices he had held, and, in 1534, fled from France. After many wanderings, he finally sought refuge in Basel, in northern Switzerland. Here he published the first edition of his *Institutes of the Christian Religion,* dedicating it to King Francis I, with a strong plea for the new faith. The first edition (1536) was in Latin, but in 1541 a French translation was published. Calvin reëdited the work a number of times, his last edition appearing in 1559.

Calvin was only twenty-seven years of age when he published the first edition of his *Institutes,* manifesting therefore a most astonishing maturity and genius. In the work he succeeded in summing up the whole of Protestant Christian doctrine and practice. The ablest treatise that the so-called reformation produced, its power was recognized by friend and foe alike. No theological exposition since the *Summa* of Aquinas had so profound an influence or gained so lasting a fame. In it Calvin placed French prose for the first time on a high level. A Renaissance scholar, he followed the classic models and wrote a book which in conciseness, in clarity of style, and perhaps in readableness had seldom been equaled. Many scholars today consider the work "a French classic."

Calvin's *Institutes* had power chiefly because of the ideas expressed. In them he regarded justification by faith as the sole way of salvation. He maintained that the only priesthood was the priesthood of all believers, and that all ministers were spiritually equal. He also denied the sacrificial character of the mass and all that was connected with purgatory. Calvin agreed with most of his fellow Protestant reformers in expressing these views. At the same time he showed strong peculiarities of emphasis and individuality of presentation.

It is probably true that "there is not one original thought in any of Calvin's works." Ample authority in the writings of his predecessors can be found to support most of his beliefs. Like the other reformers he wanted to restore the early Christian church and to demolish the "wayward" medieval institution. Recognizing the Bible as his only standard he was influenced by the early church fathers, such as Augustine, and later by Martin Luther and other Protestant leaders, in his interpretation of the Holy Book.

The supremacy of God constituted Calvin's fundamental belief. Profoundly convinced that the church was an organization of Christians entirely distinct from the state, he asserted that its members owed obedience in matters of religion only to God and to his word. They were subject to no secular control. An overwhelming sense of the Divine Majesty and of the duty of man to submit to God's will stood behind Calvin's arguments. In the light of that thought, even more than was the case with other Protestant leaders, all of his theology was molded. According to Calvin, God's sovereignty had its chief manifestation as far as the destiny of the human race was concerned, in election and in reprobation, both of which depend upon the sovereign will of God. Regarding every man, Calvin claimed, God has a definite, individual, and unchangeable purpose of salvation or of loss; and the ultimate reason for that purpose in any particular case is that God wills it so to be. In other words, God's acts were purely arbitrary; he foreknew and predestined the fate of every man from the beginning; he damned and saved irrespective of foreseen merit. "God's eternal decree" Calvin himself called "frightful."

Calvin suggested a way by which men could feel certain that they were among the elect, destined for heaven rather than for hell. This was moral behavior. Those who by their conduct satisfied the will of God were of the elect—certain of salvation. The highest virtue, he said, was faith, a matter more of the heart than of reason. Having faith, the Christian could turn to the word of God, "infallible and inerrant," as found in the Bible, and thus "seek God in his word."

Calvin used the Bible as a rigid moral law to be fulfilled to the letter by those who wanted to be of the elect. In that he differed from Luther, the German reformer. The latter, who was less ascetic and severe than Calvin, thought that everything could be left in the church which had not been prohibited by the Bible. Calvin, on the contrary, asserted that nothing should remain in the church which had not been authorized by the Holy Book. This explains the difference in the religious services of the Calvinists and of the Lutherans.

Calvin had his own ideas concerning the sacraments. He considered them to be "witnesses of the grace of God declared to us by external symbols." [1] Having no magical quality, they merely serve, he said, to confirm God's promise to us. In regard to the Lord's Supper, or the Eucharist, Calvin stood between Luther and the Swiss reformer, Zwingli, holding with the latter that Christ's words, "this is my body," are symbolic rather than literal, but inclining strongly toward the Lutheran emphasis

[1] The seven sacraments of the Roman Catholic church were: baptism, confirmation, penance, the Eucharist or Holy Communion, extreme unction, matrimony, and ordination.

upon the presence of the Lord in the Supper. That presence, Calvin believed, is not physical, but a presence of spiritual power, "on account of which those who partake of the Supper in faith, and those only, receive from it Christ's benefits."

Calvin shared with such religious leaders as Wyclif, Huss, and Zwingli, the view that the Holy Catholic church was "the whole number of the elect." While the elect constitute the church known to God, he said, the church as known to man's imperfect discrimination is the visible association composed of those "who by confession of faith, regularity of conduct, and participation in the sacraments, unite with us in acknowledging the same God and Christ." The whole number thus united, he continued, is the visible universal church. At the same time the members who are grouped in particular villages, towns, or countries, are called churches, each possessing a governmental unity. The officers of these congregations, Calvin taught, are those designated by Christ and by the apostles. They are pastors and teachers whose work may be expressed as that of the pastoral office, lay elders to assist in discipline, and deacons to care for the poor. Entrance to the ministry, he said, is by two-fold call—an inward impulse toward the office, and an invitation from the church. In other words, Calvin declared that ministers were legitimately called, "when those who may have seemed fit are elected on consent and approbation of the people."

The effect of this doctrine of the right of the local congregation to share in the choice of its minister and hence of his responsibility to it has been considered important in the development of popular liberty. Lutheranism early abandoned a somewhat similar position for dependence upon autocratic princes. The Anglican movement under Henry VIII and Elizabeth likewise had no place for this principle. Calvin, however, adopted Zwingli's idea that obedience ceases when rulers command anything contrary to God. Consequently the vigorous and practical assertion of the rights of the Christian congregation proved to be an important force in paving the way for political as well as religious freedom.

It was not difficult for Calvinists to justify their opposition to secular rulers. If ministers are chosen, they said, then they are responsible to those by whom they are elected. If spiritual rulers are responsible to those whom they serve why should not temporal magistrates, even kings, be dependent upon the will of the people. This was the interpretation placed upon Calvin's ideas by most of his followers. It is true that he did not draw these conclusions in their fullness. His French, his Dutch, his Scotch, his English, and his American followers, influenced as we shall see by a number of motives in their desire to abolish absolutism and to substitute popular control, were able to interpret Calvin's views in such a way as to give religious sanction to their opposition to autocracy and to their struggles for freedom.

In his *Institutes,* Calvin was primarily interested in establishing a well-organized church and in creating a "City of God." From the beginning he planned a theocracy in which church and state would be independent, yet in harmonious coöperation. The civil ruler's first duty was to aid the church and to preserve its purity by punishing heretics and other offenders. In this respect Calvin's views resembled those of the Roman Catholic church, except that his congregations were republican bodies in the government of which laymen fully shared. Despite this democratic tendency in organization, Calvin's church was autocratic inasmuch as it was based on one book, his *Institutes,* which was considered infallible.

This centralization of authority does much to account for the stability and for the spread of the belief.

In his plan to establish his Christian church, one peculiarity generally associated with Calvinism as it spread throughout the world stands out. This was the emphasis he laid on the cultivation and enforcement of a strenuous morality. According to Calvin, the elect were not merely called to forgiveness, but were "called into holiness." The natural man cannot himself do good works; he is totally depraved. The renewed man must do good works by the power of God's grace working in him. Enforcing thus the necessity of a strict morality, Calvin emphasized the worth of church censure. He believed it to be the chief duty of this religious organization to discipline offenders for their own good and that of the church. Discipline, he taught, was one of the chief gifts entrusted to the church for the training of its members. Discipline became, in a much higher degree than in most Protestant countries, a characteristic of those that bore Calvin's impress.

Calvin's doctrine of the elect was important in another way. It did much to encourage the development of individualism, the outstanding characteristic of the Renaissance. Salvation or damnation, Calvin asserted, was based on an individual relationship to the plan of God. Man, himself, had to work out his own salvation. Neither king, priest, nor minister could save him. He, alone, must experience those internal changes which would enable him, "called into holiness," to be of the elect—if God willed.

There was a moral grandeur [writes Preserved Smith], in the complete abandon to God and in the earnestness that was willing to sacrifice all to his will. And if we judge the tree by its fruits, at its best it brought forth a strong and good race. The noblest examples are not the theologians,

Calvin and Knox, not only drunk with God but drugged with him, much less politicians like Henry of Navarre and William of Orange, but the rank and file of the Huguenots of France, the Puritans of England, "the choice and sifted seed wherewith God sowed the wilderness" of America. These men bore themselves with I know not what of lofty seriousness, and with a matchless disdain of all mortal peril and all earthly grandeur. Believing themselves chosen vessels and elect instruments of grace, they could neither be seduced by carnal pleasure nor awed by human might. Taught that they were kings by the election of God and priests by the imposition of his hands, they despised the puny and vicious monarchs of this earth. They remained, in fact, what they always felt themselves to be, an élite, "the chosen few." [2]

GENEVA IN THE TIME OF CALVIN

About the time that the first edition of the *Institutes* was coming from the press (1536) Calvin obtained his earliest opportunity to put his ideas into practice. After he had finished the great work he made a rapid journey to Italy, visiting a sympathetic princess, Renée, duchess of Ferrara. His sojourn in Italy was brief. Inquisitorial opposition forced him to hasten to Noyon. Here Calvin was joined by a sister and a brother who gladly consented to settle with him in Strassburg or in Basel. Since warlike threatenings blocked the direct route to these places, Calvin passed through Geneva.

This city lies at the southwest end of Lake Leman, at a place where its beautiful blue waters run into those of the Rhone. Located on the most frequented of the Alpine passes, it was a center through which flowed the commerce between France, the Germanies, and Italy. Aware of Geneva's strategic position, its neighbors, the king of France, the city of Berne, and the duke of Savoy,

[2] Smith, *The Age of the Reformation*, 167-168.

desired very much to obtain possession. Internal difficulties, also, invited intervention.

By the end of the fifteenth century Geneva, a town of 16,000 inhabitants, was a center of trade, of pleasure, and of piety. Its government was shared by three powers, the bishop, the *vidame*, representing the duke of Savoy, and the councils, representing the people. Inasmuch as each authority coveted complete control, a slight dispute threatened to disturb at any time the unstable equilibrium they maintained.

During the first part of the sixteenth century a patriotic movement appeared in Geneva. Determined to be free, the citizens engaged in a desperate attempt to overthrow the authority of the house of Savoy and of the bishop. A crisis occurred in 1526, when Geneva, having denounced the authority of Savoy, arranged a league for mutual protection with the neighboring city states of Freiburg and of Berne. Meanwhile the citizens denounced the authority of the pope, expelled the bishop, and broke up religious houses. The arrival, in 1532, of William Farel, the reformer from Berne, did much to precipitate these attacks on the Catholic church. Another crisis was reached when in May, 1536, Farel got the Genevans to renounce the Catholic religion.

The way was now prepared for the establishment of an independent republic. But who was to lead in the movement? Certain military commanders from Berne tried to answer that question by attempting to make Geneva dependent upon their city. They failed. The citizens of Geneva were determined that Geneva, including nearly thirty dependent villages nearby, should be recognized as an independent republic. The fiery Farel was the logical man to end the political and religious strife by establishing this democratic government. He realized that he lacked organizing ability, and wisely decided that another leader must be found. At this moment, according to Farel, he received a message which he believed was sent by God.

In the evening of a July day in 1536, three tired strangers entered the city, looking for a place to spend the night. As they walked along the streets, someone recognized Calvin and informed Farel of this fact. Immediately Farel found Calvin and begged the latter to help the work of God which he had begun in Geneva. Calvin, like many academic persons, refused at first, claiming that he preferred the life of a scholar to that of an administrator. Farel was determined. Threatening to ask God to curse Calvin's scholastic plans, Farel caused the Frenchman to assent to his suggestion in order, probably, to avoid further complications. Having accepted the invitation, Calvin prepared to make the most of it.

In 1536, Calvin and Farel presented to the city councils a *Confession of Faith* and a *Catechism* for individual adoption by all citizens. In submitting the *Catechism* these leaders were perhaps the first to recognize the importance of enabling each man "to account for the faith that is in him."

Calvin then demonstrated his ability as an organizer. Preparing his famous articles for the government of the new church, based largely on the principles found in his *Institutes,* he laid them before the civil authorities, receiving their prompt approval. But many citizens were not so enthusiastic. Personally they resented his emphasis upon moral rectitude, and as patriots they opposed him because he was a foreigner. At that time there were many pleasure-loving people in Geneva, who were fond of dancing, of music, and of masquerades. As they understood Calvin's proposals, all this was to be abandoned, and a "holy reign of terror" was to be substituted. These citizens, who had fought for independence against the duke and the bishop, did not propose to see their hard-won liberty lost as a result of a new tyranny, imposed by a puritanical, alien administrator. They refused to give up their many pleasures. They were not interested in this medieval concept of Utopia. They preferred to imitate the pagans and to enjoy life. Calvin's plans to establish his church, to rule the city, and to regulate society were rejected. The Genevans were not willing to have their city shaped into a veritable city of God in which men would work and pray—not play.

Calvin was indignant when he heard of this opposition. Discovering that some of them were "undesirables," or representatives of Geneva's underworld, Calvin cleverly called all of them libertines, just as many orthodox bourgeois citizens today characterize their personal or political enemies as bolshevists, or anarchists. In February, 1538, the elections to the city council went against Calvin and Farel. A crisis was reached when the town council decided to adopt the method of celebrating the Eucharist used at Berne. Calvin and Farel were now angry and refused to obey. This opposition resulted in a riot at the Lord's table and their expulsion by the city government.

Calvin went to Strassburg, where he met Bucer, another reformer, republished his *Institutes*, and married Idelette de Bure, the widow of an Anabaptist—"a grave and honorable woman." Their married life, while "correct, helpful, and happy," was not of long duration. His wife, an invalid for some time, died in 1549. The only child, a son, was taken away in infancy. Calvin never married again. After 1549 he allowed no "worldly interest" to interfere with "God's plans."

During Calvin's exile matters went from bad to worse in Geneva. The party which had brought about the banishment of Farel and Calvin became unpopular by negotiating a treaty with Berne, unfavorable so far as the interests of Geneva were concerned. Finally the group in sympathy with Calvin succeeded in overthrowing the opposition and in influencing the city council to recall Calvin.

The French reformer at first seemed unwilling to accept the invitation, but he consented, saying: "I thought the matter over conscientiously and with reverence, and when I saw it was my duty, I gave way and consented to return to the flock from which I had been, as it were, torn away." Wisely Calvin refused to yield unconditionally. It was well understood that upon his return he should have full sway in establishing his church in Geneva.

Upon his arrival, September 12, 1541, Calvin became the "mainspring of the Genevese republic. He set all its wheels in motion." Nominally he held no official position, usurping none of the powers of government, although he influenced their exercise. Actually he made the laws, while the civil councils and authorities confirmed them and carried them out. In civil matters Calvin took the part of an advisor and not a magistrate. "His power was that of spirit," says one writer. "It was the force of intellect, of persuasion, and of will; but it was none the less compelling." Calvin was virtually a dictator.

By means of this position he was able to make Geneva a city after his own heart. The form of government he established was a strict theocracy. Both church and state, Calvin believed, were necessary "to the good ordering of society." All human authority was the creation of God. His will had formed the state to care for the temporal man, and the church to care for the immortal man. Over the state God placed the magistrates, who might be an emperor, a king, or a syndic or council, created by the people for the people. Whatever the ruler might be, he was still a power ordained by God for the good of men and for the regulation of society. The ministers were responsible to the state in all civil matters; but the magistrates were accountable to the church in all religious questions, especially those affecting faith and conduct. The laws of the state were civil in form, but religious in their origin; the laws of the church were civil in sanction, though spiritual in scope and in purpose.

Guided by these ideas, Calvin proceeded to establish his system of government and of discipline by creating a definite religious organization, designed to coöperate with the secular authorities in the governing of Geneva. Advised by his ministers and by six sympathetic laymen of the Genevan councils he set forth his plan in his *Ordinances ecclésiastiques.* These became with some modification the religious constitution of the Genevan church.

This remarkable constitution can be understood only in the light of Calvin's emphasis upon discipline as essential to church nurture, and upon the right of the laity to share in church government. The clergy of the city met in a body known as the congregation, "a venerable company" which discussed and prepared legislation for the consideration of the consistory. In this larger group, in addition to the clergy, the laity was represented by twelve elders chosen by the council, not by the people at large. The church and state "were thus completely identified in a highly aristocratic polity."

At first Calvin favored as the best form of government either aristocracy or a mixture of aristocracy and democracy, "such as the Lord established among the people of Israel," he said. After sixteen more years of observations on the "imperfections of man" he changed his political ideas. He now favored constitutional government in the hands of the many, ". . . so that if anyone arrogate to himself more than is right, the many may act as censors and masters to restrain his ambition."

At the close of his career Calvin favored representative government "by common consent," in both church and state, as "the best condition by far." He also stated that when men became kings by hereditary right "this does not seem consistent with liberty." Aroused by the oppression of his followers by autocratic kings in France and in the Spanish Netherlands, Calvin, before his death, advanced the theory of constitutional resistance through divinely appointed representatives, responsible to God and to the people. Such resistance on the part of estates or parliaments was constitutional and rational, because it was based on the word of God (the Bible), a political covenant or compact (preferably written), a coronation oath, and some form of fundamental law.

In Geneva, Calvin remained until his death an uncrowned king, bent upon one thing—the creation of a society of saints. This was the object of his ecclesiastical ordinances. "The Bible was adopted as the norm." All persons were to conform to the precepts found in the Holy Book, excepting the Jewish ceremonies which were considered abrogated by the New Testament. To see that the citizens lived holy lives, Geneva was divided into sections. Elders, assigned to the various quarters, visited every house at least once a year and investigated the actions, the speech, and the opinions of the inmates.

Calvin was not satisfied with this substitute for the Catholic inquisitorial courts. A multitude of spies kept the consistory informed at all times as to the conduct of the citizens. Anything that could be construed as an attack upon the church or as a departure from the rigid discipline maintained by Calvin was enough to bring a man under suspicion and finally under arrest. The elders sat as a regular court, hearing complaints, examining witnesses, and inflicting spiritual punishments, such as public censure, penance, excommunication, or forcing the culprit to beseech pardon on his knees in church. When the consistory considered it necessary, it could invoke the aid of the civil courts. The latter usually handled crimes, such as adultery, blasphemy, witchcraft, and heresy, dealing out astonishingly and increasingly drastic sentences. In the sixteenth century, punishments were heavier than they are now. Calvin was not alone in advocating harsh treatment for crimes which would, at the present time, receive light penalties, if any at all.

The low moral conditions in Geneva explain, even though they fail to justify, Calvin's methods. When he rose to power in that city, luxurious and even riotous living was not uncommon. To make matters worse, it was claimed that many clergymen and monks, as well as members of distinguished families, were far from setting an elevated example to their less conspicuous neighbors. Among the lower classes ignorance and vice abounded. Men and women, it was said, knew no shame, and sought no privacy. Reckless gambling, adultery, and blasphemy made up the common sights and sounds of the day and of the night. Prostitution was sanctioned by the state, and a woman having the title "Queen of the Brothel" superintended that ancient profession. Apparently the forces of evil in Calvin's day were about the same as they are now.

The Genevan dictator was a reformer *par excellence.* Many today think as he did, but few can equal his achievements. Sick in the flesh as a result of chronic headaches and indigestion, but strong in spirit, Calvin would not even consider a compromise with the devil. All sin, he said, was to be blotted out, in order that his followers should be of the elect. Adultery was punished with death; a child was beheaded for having struck its parent; banishment, imprisonment, even drowning were inflicted on those convicted of unchastity; to sing a lewd song was a crime; to laugh at Calvin's sermons was a crime; to invite too many guests to a feast, or to serve too many courses was a crime; everybody was to attend public worship; everybody was forced to partake of the Lord's Supper. Men, women, and children were punished for not doing certain things, and for doing other things. Punishments for various offences were anything but infrequent. Between 1542 and 1546 there were, in this town of 16,000 souls, no less than 58 executions and 76 banishments.

To what extent was Geneva purified as a result of Calvin's discipline? By forcing men and women to obey his numerous laws, designed to prevent them from working or playing on Sundays, from dancing at any time, from going to theaters, from playing cards, from cursing, and from drinking, Calvin certainly gave to Genevan citizens considerable opportunity to lead pure and holy lives. But did Geneva become a moral Utopia? According to John Knox and other followers who visited the city, Geneva "was the most perfect school of Christ that ever was on earth since the days of the apostles." An examination of the acts of the consistory indicates that this was not exactly correct. The records show the existence of vice in Geneva long after Calvin came into power. It is true that in time the Puritan element did manage to dominate the city, because most of the weak and wicked brothers and sisters were either driven out or executed. Consequently Geneva almost became a "perfect" school of Christ, because of the fact that only the devout were allowed to live there. Moreover, those who immigrated to Geneva, taking the places of those who moved out, were men of austere minds, drawn thither seeking refuge from persecution elsewhere, or by the desire to sit at the feet of the great reformer. Here they were able to worship God in their own fashion, as long as their way was Calvin's way. But they did not mind Calvin's vigorous rule. They, themselves, were outcasts and had no easy, happy golden days of long ago to remember, as had the native Genevese. They were preparing for the future when they, the elect, would be able to enjoy "everlasting happiness."

OPPOSITION TO CALVIN: THE LIBERTINES

Calvin's work, nevertheless, was met by strenuous opposition. His severe discipline and the growing influence of foreigners aroused the hostility of the old Genevan families. Sincere disbelievers in his doctrines and radical sects, which rose out of the religious revolts, added their weight to the opposition Calvin had to overcome. The determined Frenchman was adamant. Finally he succeeded in having the majority of these opponents condemned to death. Most of them avoided this punishment by flight.

Religious opposition constituted a difficult problem. One group, opposing Calvin, was called the libertines, a word which Calvin had applied to his enemies for some time. At first this term meant something like "freethinker" today, and later it gained a more unsavory connotation. In Calvin's day these libertines were, as a rule, men who viewed personality, or individual characteristics, as a mere passing manifestation of the one God, who is all and does all. Sin had for them no real existence; and salvation or forgiveness they conceived as simply the recognition that all actions, whether man calls them good or bad, are simply God's work.

To Calvin these were the ideas of the devil. He turned

his heavy artillery on these exponents of evil, advocating death as the only fitting punishment. One of these libertines, James Gruet, by name, was especially distasteful to Calvin. Gruet had the audacity to post on the pulpit of St. Peter's Church at Geneva a warning to Calvin, in no uncertain terms, to leave the city. Moreover, he had written on one of Calvin's tracts the words "all rubbish." This in itself was a mortal sin. So Gruet was quickly arrested. After frightful torture on the rack, in an attempt to make him incriminate others, he was tried for heresy, convicted, sentenced to death for blasphemy, and beheaded (1547). After Gruet's death Calvin apparently considered it necessary to justify further this act. He announced that Gruet had said that "Jesus Christ was a good-for-nothing liar, and a false seducer, and that he (Gruet) denied the existence of God and immortality." Poor Gruet was not in a position to reply to these remarks, but it is known that before his death he called "on God as his Lord."

This tyrannical act on the part of Calvin produced a reaction. The libertines became angry. They called Calvin, Cain. But opposition only served to increase Calvin's fanaticism, and, as a result, he committed perhaps the most regrettable act of his career.

About 1553, a famous Spanish physician, Michael Servetus, published a book at Vienne setting forth his ideas about the Trinity, "which he compared to the three-headed monster, Cerberus, but admitting the divinity of Christ." He also denied the doctrine of original sin, and asserted that baptism should be for adults only. It appears that Calvin and Servetus were entirely familiar with each other's views: at one time they had planned to have a public debate on the doctrine of the Trinity. But it was not held because Servetus, wisely perhaps, failed to appear. Meanwhile the discussion by letters became exceedingly bitter, Calvin going so far as to warn the Spaniard not to come to Geneva. "If you do," he said, "I shall exert whatever influence I may have to prevent you from going forth alive."

After that warning Servetus should have left Calvin strictly alone. Instead, he sent him his publication *The Restitution of Christianity* (1553). In this work he assailed with equal rigor the Roman Catholic dogmas and the teachings of Protestant Christianity. He was arrested at once. To avoid death at the hands of the state, after conviction by the Catholic church, Servetus escaped from prison, thanks to assistance given to him by some of his wealthy patients. Meanwhile the church carried out his trial, and he was consumed by fire in effigy.

For three months Servetus did a wise thing. He remained in hiding. Then he made his fatal mistake; he suddenly appeared among the congregation in the cathedral at Geneva, while Calvin was preaching. The law now took its course. Servetus was arrested, imprisoned, and accused of heresy.

Calvin's followers demanded a quick conviction and punishment. Calvin said that while he hoped that the court would sentence Servetus to death, he wanted the sentence carried out with as little cruelty as possible. The court found the Spanish physician guilty and ordered him to the stake. Farel arrived in time to be present at the burning, walking beside the prisoner and trying to get him to recant. But the unhappy Servetus showed no signs of repentance, crying, "God preserve my soul! O Jesus, Son of the eternal God, have mercy on me!" He was burned alive on October 26, 1553. "Farel called on the bystanders to witness that the above words uttered by the dying man showed that he was still in the power of Satan." No one present considered it advisable to disagree with Farel.

By 1555 the power of the libertines was completely broken and Calvin ruled Geneva with a rod of iron until his death in 1564. Worn out with labor and ill health, this religious leader, who claimed to be a chosen vessel of God, this determined man with a cold heart and a hot temper, finally handed over his work to his successor, Theodore Beza (1519-1605), "a man after his own heart." Beza lacked Calvin's creative genius and his strength of will. Therefore the city council was able gradually to free itself from spiritual tyranny. Towards the end of the century the pastors had lost much of their political power. Geneva remained, nevertheless, a center of learning and of industry, as well as a model of Calvinistic discipline.

GENEVA, CENTER OF AN INTERNATIONAL RELIGION

By 1564, Geneva was the center of an international religion. Even before his death Calvin was able to look beyond the gates of his city and to see evidences of his international power and reputation. Geneva, indeed, had become the capital of a great branch of Protestantism. Its mandates were now issued to all of the countries in western Europe. Italian, Spanish, English, Dutch, Scotch, and French followers thronged to this city to learn the laws of a new type of Christianity. In all parts of Europe, claims an enthusiastic Protestant writer, "images, vestments, organs, bells, candles, and rituals were thrown away, and in their places appeared plain meeting houses, in which men and women engaged in Bible-reading, hymns, and prayers, and then listened to long and often depressing sermons."

As an international religion Calvinism even influenced the doctrines and ceremonies of other sects, among them, the Anglican church. Perhaps, if Calvin were alive today, he would account for the popularity of his belief by claiming that inasmuch as it was the true religion it naturally appealed to people everywhere. More logical reasons can be given. Calvin's revolt was more thorough, militant, and aggressive than was Luther's. "His gift for organization and the pains he took to train ministers and apostles also accounts for the success of his religion." Moreover, unlike Lutheranism, his church was not subordinate to civil authority. To Calvin it was a sacramental, aristocratic organization, with an authoritative ministry. Like Catholicism it was above the state and thus international in its scope.

There are those, however, who see in the economic, the political, and social changes in western Europe the real explanation for the remarkable spread and strength of Calvinism.

ECONOMIC SIGNIFICANCE OF CALVINISM

While Calvin was preaching in Geneva, an economic transformation was taking place in Europe, even deeper and more enduring in its consequences than the religious revolt. This was the Commercial Revolution—a revolt which greatly facilitated the rise of capitalism and of the middle classes, and which made possible the transition from the dominance of agriculture to that of commerce. Geneva was one of the first of the great cities to profit by this revolution. Before Calvin's day the city was a place consisting of narrow, ill-paved, and filthy streets. The construction of the houses and the habits of the people disregarded the most elementary laws of sanitation. Sickness was rife in the city and plagues were frequent. Despite these unsanitary conditions, the city hummed with life. Four times a year great fairs were held in which Spaniards, Provençals, Normans, and men from

Flanders rubbed shoulders and bargained with men of Geneva, Milan, Venice, and Tuscany. The streets in front of the houses were lined with booths in which were piled groceries, silks, furs, gold, jewelry, armor, and many other goods. Between the fairs there was always a large import and export trade going on. In the workshops men were busy, and the sound of the hammer, saw, and the loom could be heard throughout the day.

Money was plentiful and freely spent by the pleasure-loving Genevans. They wore gorgeous clothing, and held magnificent banquets. Laws were frequently passed to check extravagances, but with little success. With the exception of the bishops, few tried to be aristocratic. Indeed, men of the upper classes worked along with the commoners in the various enterprises, and like them went to the market for their own supplies.

Into this city of pleasure, of licence, of wealth, and of intrigue came John Calvin, determined to establish his city of God. When the citizens realized that Calvin intended to deprive them of the many pleasures they had enjoyed for years, they revolted and expelled him. But they soon discovered that he was the one man who could unify them and thus save them from foreign intervention and internal chaos. Moreover, they knew that without security and peace they could not carry on commerce and enjoy prosperity. Therefore they recalled Calvin, and suffered loss of personal liberty in order to check those forces which threatened to deprive them of economic power as well as of political freedom.

Calvin's administration justified their support. The sober, discreet, and industrious bourgeois citizens who remained in Geneva benefited materially as well as spiritually as a result of his reign. He established law and order, maintained prosperity, and indirectly justified the pursuit of gold. They were satisfied.

Calvin did not consciously advance views of economic significance. His beliefs just happened to "fit in" with the economic changes ushered in by the Commercial Revolution. Furthermore, Calvin was reactionary and as such he accidentally expressed views which later took on economic significance. Determined to revive what he considered "the original church," many of his ideas constitute his interpretation of the views of the early Christian fathers. He accepted, for example, two great ideals which characterized early monastic asceticism. These were: the leading of a sober, frugal, industrious life, and the unremitting, indefatigable pursuit of one's calling. By these marks could be distinguished the elect and by such conduct could the Christian glorify God, and prove the fact of his own redemption.

It so happened that a sober, frugal, and a busy life usually meant that a man was of the elect in worldly goods as well as in spiritual power. Many Calvinists therefore concluded that an industrious career with few holidays and the glorification of work and of thrift, rather than of pleasure, constituted not only a sure road to heaven, but also a dependable way to economic independence. According to them Calvin placed the responsibility for economic security as well as spiritual salvation squarely upon the shoulders of the individual. By stressing the right of this single person to work out his destiny, and by explaining the failure of the many and the success of the few by means of his doctrine of predestination, Calvin actually justified economic as well as religious individualism. This religious approval of economic activity explains perhaps why "most of the shining lights of Calvinism arose from the mercantile classes," and why "among Calvinists, business ability and piety have always gone together."

POLITICAL AND INTELLECTUAL SIGNIFICANCE OF CALVINISM

Calvin's works at Geneva had political and educational as well as economic significance. It is true that so far as Geneva was concerned he established an aristocratic theocracy in which he was a dictator. Moreover, in subordinating the state to the church, Calvin was wholly medieval. At the same time, in emphasizing the supremacy of God and the right of resistance to all other authority, if necessary to do God's work, he did much to curb the powers of kings and to increase the authority of the elected representatives of the people. There is little that is new in Calvin's political ideas. Thomas Aquinas and the Jesuits justified opposition to kings who opposed the church and thereby the people. Calvin, by presenting these ideas clearly and logically, by justifying them by the scriptures, and by extending participation in the church government to laymen, gave a religious sanction to the various political movements which paved the way through local parish governments to our modern constitutional monarchies and republics. He acknowledged the right of the individual to remove the magistrate who disobeys the word of God. He implied the right of the individual to determine whether or not the word of God has been disobeyed. Consequently he justified many revolutionary leaders in their belief that God gave them the right to oppose tyranny.

Calvin's work at Geneva also had educational significance. To be saved, said Calvin, a man must carry out God's will expressed in the Bible. But to discover God's will one must be able to read the Holy Book. Therefore Calvin, assisted by two educators, published in 1538 a prospectus of the Genevan elementary schools. This work emphasized three educational ideas: (1) careful grammatical drill before rhetorical display; (2) a substantial provision for teaching both the vernacular and practical arithmetic; (3) training for civil as well as ecclesiastical leadership. Education in "Calvin's Biblical Commonwealth" was a logical necessity for both laymen and ministers. He made the public school a definite part of the training of youth, working out a system of primary, secondary, and university education which served as a training school and model for his followers throughout the world.

To understand Calvinism one must not stop with a study of his work in Geneva. This so-called city of God, as it was formed and fashioned by the untiring, unbending will of a frail, sick man, was but the beginning. The movement soon spread throughout the world and achieved international importance.

Chapter II

CALVINISM AND THE FRENCH RELIGIOUS WARS

FRANCE IN THE SIXTEENTH CENTURY

The sixteenth century has already been characterized as an age of transition. It was a period of instability, of rapidly changing concepts, of widening vistas, and of unprecedented innovations. Europe was speedily losing its medieval aspects and assuming those of the modern world. This century opened auspiciously for France. She had recovered from the effects of the war with England. Her devastated fields were again cultivated, her population was increasing, and a growing commerce indicated an era of prosperity. She was ready to adopt the intellectual ideas of the Renaissance and to participate in the spread of western culture.

The French campaigns in Italy, inaugurated during the latter part of the fifteenth century, were indicative of the strength of the French monarchy. Important internal problems had been solved by that time, and the government was now able to institute an aggressive foreign policy. The invasions of Italy stimulated the minds of Frenchmen, even though they did not add to their earthly possessions. It is true that the French did not need this outside stimulus, because France was awakening itself. Nevertheless, contact with Italy greatly hastened the remarkable, spontaneous, intellectual activity which characterized the reign of Francis I (1515-1547).

Francis I was a popular and a powerful king. At that time the monarch had taken over considerable authority into his own hands. Thanks to the development of commerce and of industry he had money enough to hire an army. This enabled him to enforce the laws, and to break, or at least to curb, the power of the nobles. He was no longer dependent for support upon the vague pledges of his vassals. Furthermore, the king of France had become the symbol of unity against the external enemies of the nation. He represented and controlled the might of the state. The Italian wars, which began in 1494, and the conflicts with the Hapsburgs, which followed, demonstrated his power. Favored by his location on the inner line of defense, by his centralized government, by his control of the army and of finance, and by his influence over the church, he checked the ambitions of Charles V and "provided the states of Europe with a bulwark against the menace of a general absorption in the dominions of the Hapsburgs."

The power of the king, resting primarily on the support of the bourgeois classes, was greatly increased by the concordat of 1516, arranged between the pope and Francis I. This agreement made the monarch virtually the supreme head of a national church. By it he gained sole authority to fill all religious offices in France as they became vacant. He could appoint laymen to church benefices, and was able not only to control the vast wealth of that institution, but also to reward his favorites with ecclesiastical positions. Dominant in matters of church and state, the king of France now had, in theory at least, the authority of Cæsar. He even had visions of creating another Latin empire and of making Paris the successor to Rome.

Despite his great authority, Francis I was not an absolute ruler. Politically, France was a semi-popular, semi-autocratic kingdom. The rights of the people, especially of the nobility and of the clergy, were asserted by the Estates General which met from time to time, and by the high courts of justice. These latter organizations were called *parlements*. They were powerful because of their right to register new laws. The most notable was that of Paris.

Various groups were desirous of regaining many rights which, in their opinion, had been illegally taken from them. The nobles who still retained considerable personal power, were only too eager to take advantage of any situation that would enable them to recover their feudal prerogatives at the expense of the king. The clergy of high rank were conservatives. Drawn from aristocratic families, they naturally sided with the nobles in meetings of the Estates General. Unprivileged classes, on the other hand, were always willing to avail themselves of any chance to weaken the nobility. At the same time they tried to avoid paying the heavy taxes levied by the government. England and Spain also had territorial ambitions in France, and the church bitterly resented the interference of the government in its affairs. When a number of weak kings ascended the throne and Protestantism entered France, the restless elements used the religious wars as a means to further their own interests.

PROTESTANTISM IN FRANCE

In the history of French Protestantism, political as well as religious persecution played a large part. During the first half of the sixteenth century the attack upon the Catholic church was inaugurated by the Christian humanists, especially by Lefèvre. Wishing to purify the church by setting aside "good works" in favor of "justification by faith," he tried to create a group of followers who would preach Christ "simply with the aim of touching the heart, not of dazzling the mind." The Christian humanists who wanted to reform the church were followed (shortly after Francis I became king) by Lutherans who entered France and established a Protestant organization. Francis I, backed by the Sorbonne and the *Parlement* of Paris, opposed them. Determined to maintain his control over a unified church and state, he commanded the Catholic clergy to "proceed against" all followers of Luther.

Opposition seemed to encourage the spread of the reform movement in France. At first it was bourgeois, the important centers being Paris, Meaux, and Lyons, and its chief adherents merchants and artisans. At the same time many intellectuals secretly studied and supported the movement. These individuals expected the favor of the liberal Francis I. The king, however, was interested in the pagan, not the Christian Renaissance. The brilliant court in which he maintained a patronage of literature, the arts, and learning indicated his desire to renew the classical past by making Paris another Rome and the French king another Cæsar.

Queen Margaret of Navarre, talented sister of Francis I, became a devotee of the Christian rather than of the pagan Renaissance. Living in the small southern kingdom of her second husband, Henry d'Albret, king of Navarre, she corresponded with a number of reformers, including Luther, and wrote *The Mirror of the Sinful Soul* "in the best style of penitent piety." Calvin, at one time, had high hopes of winning her to his church, but was disappointed. "Her house," he then decided, "harbored servants of the devil rather than the family of Jesus Christ."

The French Lutherans were not successful in their attempts to spread the new faith. This was largely due to lack of royal support. In the Germanies the rulers backed Luther in order to bring the church under their control. In France, however, the king had virtually made the Catholic church a state institution. Therefore, he opposed the establishment of the Lutheran sect. In his opinion, it would weaken rather than strengthen his power.

Calvinism made more headway in France than Lutheranism. The publication of Calvin's *Institutes of the Christian Religion* (1536) gave all French Protestants a much needed leader and standard. Henceforth the Calvinists dominated French Protestantism, becoming a well-organized and influential minority in France.

The Calvinists, called Huguenots, a term of obscure origin, soon established a definite theological system and a militant church organization which the French Protestants had earlier lacked. This religious organization appealed to certain individuals. Aware of the political possibilities of the new religion, many members of the middle classes became Protestants, planning to use the religious party as a means of opposing the nobles as well as the monarch. Before long the Huguenots threatened to create a state within a state. Consequently, involved in politics, they had to defend themselves against the attacks of the monarch and the Catholic church.

Francis I was unable to continue a rigorous policy of oppression. Because of his opposition to the Hapsburgs, he was forced to arrange an alliance with the German Lutherans. The latter demanded that in return for their support he tolerate their French co-religionists. Accordingly, Francis I, in 1535, published an edict ordering the persecution to cease.

On his death, his son, Henry II (1547-1559), became king. Henry was a big man physically, but was weak intellectually. Uninterested in culture, he devoted most of his time to various forms of exercise. The new queen was Catherine de' Medici, daughter of Lorenzo II de'

Medici of Florence. Disliked at first by the French people because she was a foreigner, she meddled very little during her husband's régime in matters of state.

At this time the government of France fell largely into the hands of two powerful families—the house of Montmorency and the house of Guise. The Montmorencys exercised great influence during Henry's reign, chiefly through the military and diplomatic abilities of their leader, the constable Anne of Montmorency. Banished shortly before the death of Francis I, Anne was restored to favor by Henry II, who became strongly attached to his loyal and ambitious subject. In 1551, Anne of Montmorency received the title of duke and peer, which made him the equal in rank of all except princes of the blood. He was now in a position to promote the interests of his family and of his relatives. Since his children were too young for promotion, he used his influence to advance his nephews, the famous Châtillon brothers, sons of his sister. The eldest, Odet, obtained a cardinal's hat; the second, Gaspard de Coligny, became admiral of France; and the youngest, D'Andelot, commanded infantry within the limits of France. Of these three brothers who later joined the Huguenot cause, Gaspard, admiral of France, was the most important. A firm friend of the king of France, and an ardent statesman and warrior, he later exerted great influence.

Opposed to the Montmorencys was the house of Guise. The great power wielded by this family owed much to the position of their estates, part of which were fiefs of the French king and part subject to the Holy Roman Empire. "As suited their convenience, they could act either as Frenchmen or as foreign nobles." Fortunate marriage alliances increased the prestige of the Guises; and when they contrived the marriage of their niece, Mary Stuart of Scotland, to Francis II, heir of Henry

II, the fortunes of the family were closely bound to those of the royal house of France. Claiming descent from Charlemagne himself, they boldly emphasized their French origin. According to their enemies, however, the ambitious members of the family were willing to subordinate all interests to their own advancement.

Military achievements help to explain their rise to power. Through the ability of Francis of Guise, France was able to obtain from Charles V, Holy Roman emperor, the three important bishoprics, Metz, Toul, and Verdun. Moreover, a conflict with England enabled the Guises to drive the English from French soil. By 1559, the Guise supremacy at court was attained. Now they planned the expulsion of their rivals the Montmorencys, and the princes of the royal house of Bourbon, Antoine (king of Navarre), and his brother, Condé. At the same time it looked as though the crown was no longer to be a factor in the government. Francis of Guise seemed destined to become a virtual dictator, or possibly king of France.

The rivalry between the Guises and the Montmorencys constituted the opening act of an important period in the history of France. During this critical time the monarchy, faced by the danger of dissolution and determined to hold its historic prerogative, strove desperately to maintain the balance of power between the two families. Happily the abdication of Charles V in 1556 and the division of his empire temporarily removed the threat against the overturn of the balance of power in Europe. France could henceforth deal with Spain and with the Holy Roman Empire as separate entities. This was indeed fortunate. It enabled France to withdraw from international affairs and to concentrate upon her critical internal problems.

Of these the religious question was, perhaps, the most

difficult to solve. The Catholic church, which would in time probably have provided the leadership necessary for a solution, was lacking in real statesmen. The best minds of the time were gradually being drawn into the vortex of secular affairs. The Middle Ages were passing and the intellectual center of gravity was shifting slowly from the religious to the political field.

The Huguenots had the enthusiasm and leaders that the old church lacked. By 1559 Calvinism had spread into southern France. Its strongholds were in the river towns, on the highways of trade, or in seaports like Rouen and La Rochelle. Normandy, on the channel, was the chief Protestant province of France. Although the great majority belonged to the artisan and middle classes, Calvinism was not restricted to these groups. It had affected several religious orders, the intellectuals, and even the aristocracy. During the reign of Henry II, in spite of rigorous oppression, Protestantism gained powerful and influential adherents from the nobility, among whom the Châtillon brothers and Louis of Bourbon, prince of Condé, were the most valuable. This new aristocratic element furnished the military leadership the Protestants needed at that time. Soon a dangerous discontent pervaded the whole realm. The terrible and cruel persecutions of the Huguenots, inaugurated by the Guises, made the Protestants desperate. "We must defend the king against the ambitious foreigners, the Guises," they said. The stage was set for the frightful civil wars.

Henry II supported the Guise oppression of the Huguenots. This sect, he sincerely believed, intended to undermine his authority. Judging from appearances he had good reason to be apprehensive. Scattered throughout the country, the Huguenots had organized churches modeled on that of Geneva. The country was divided into districts; within these districts the churches sent representatives, both clerical and lay, to a central consistory. Over the whole of the church of the entire nation there was to be a national synod, to which each consistory was to send one clergyman and one or two lay elders. The congregations and consistories constituted machinery for religious administration, for the collection of money, and for the raising of armies.

From the beginning the Huguenots disclaimed any personal ambitions. True to the teachings of Calvin, they proclaimed passive obedience to authority, as it was, they said, the business of the subject to do his duty and to leave to God the punishment of kings who failed to do theirs. Calvin, however, interpreted this idea broadly, when he heard of their oppression by the French monarch. In his communications he informed his followers in France that this passive attitude was not required of public officials whose explicit function it was to curb the power of the monarchs. He also declared that the limit of obedience to kings is the command of God. In other words, he informed his followers that their leaders could oppose the king, if the latter disobeyed the commands of God. This laid the ground-work for vigorous resistance instead of passive obedience to governmental oppression. Calvin created a church in France which was practically a republic, with an organization capable of resisting the king even though it preached submission.

Alarmed by the growth of Calvinism, Henry II was planning a drastic measure to suppress this movement when he died (1559)—"a merciful dispensation of Providence," said Calvin. His death marked the end of one period and the beginning of another. For forty years France had been absorbed in the struggle with the Hapsburgs. For the next forty years she was to be completely occupied with the wars of religion. Externally she played a weak rôle, because of civil strife and weak government. "All of her interests, both foreign and domestic, were from this time forgotten in the intensity of the passions aroused by fanaticism."

The death of Henry II also marked an important change in the evolution of the French government. Until then the trend had been from feudalism to absolutism. Indeed, the classical ideal of one faith, one law, and one ruler had been nearly attained. But now this development was checked in two ways. The great nobles, in the first place, found in Calvinism a chance to assert their privileges against the king and to restore the feudal régime. On the other hand the middle classes, especially in the cities, displayed republican tendencies. Many of them proceeded to resist not only the authority of prelates, but that of the king as well. Joined by a great number of priests who hated the inequalities of the old régime in which the high clergy had everything and the lesser clergy were very poor, these bourgeois radicals even went so far as to advocate a kind of republic. To them Calvinism taught essentially the excellence of all Christians and their equality before God.

Opposed by the exponents of feudal authority and of republicanism, the French monarchy surely was in a critical position. To aggravate the situation, Henry II was followed by three of his sons, each of them, in different degrees and ways, a weakling. Francis II was the first. A sickly boy, not quite sixteen years of age, he was completely under the control of his wife, Mary Stuart, queen of Scotland, and her uncles, Francis, duke of Guise, and the cardinal of Lorraine. The Huguenots, fearing Guise influence at court, turned to the Bourbon leaders, especially the prince of Condé and the king of Navarre, for support. Meanwhile the Guises inaugurated terrible and cruel persecutions of the Huguenots. Finally a plot, arranged by a Huguenot adventurer to rid the country of the Guise tyranny, brought about a crisis. The aim of this so-called conspiracy of Amboise (1560) was generally thought to be the extermination of the foreigners, including the Guises, and the substitution in places of authority of the princes of the blood, the house of Montmorency, and that of Châtillon. But a rumor of the plot was carried to the Guises, and prompt measures were taken to circumvent it. Unfortunately, the harsh manner in which they suppressed it served to increase the hatred, not only between the Huguenots and the Catholics, but also between the noble factions as well. The Guises, convinced of the guilt of the Montmorency and the Châtillon families, swore revenge, although it seems that Condé, not a member of either house, was the only one who could even be suspected of being implicated in the affair. The latter was the first to feel their wrath. He was foully enticed to the court, arrested, imprisoned, and convicted of treason. Happily the death of Francis II (1560) saved his life.

As the new king, Charles IX, was only nine years of age, the regency fell to his mother, Catherine de' Medici. She ruled France for thirty years. Naturally she tried to do everything in her power to protect the interests of her sons. This was not an easy thing to do. Indeed, when one considers the problems confronting the queen mother, one must admit that she did remarkably well.

Catherine de' Medici has been one of the most maligned characters in history. Undoubtedly she was open to criticism. Of huge bulk, with repulsive features, she was anything but beautiful. Moreover, she was a foreigner, an Italian. Her contemporaries, ardent Frenchmen, did not find it difficult to ridicule and to hate her. Catherine had real ability. She could wear out her followers in a rapid walk, and could generally outthink her enemies. Active of mind and of body, she also had a profound love of the beautiful. As a connoisseur and an indefatigable collector she gratified her admiration of the magnificent not only by beautiful palaces and gorgeous clothes, but also by collecting pictures, statues, tapestries, furniture, porcelain, silver, books, and manuscripts.

Catherine was also a *Politique* to her finger tips. She had neither sympathy nor patience with fanatics who would put religion or any other interest above the peace and prosperity of the state. She favored the economic development of the country through the establishment of colonies and the expansion of trade and industry. Moreover, she was determined to preserve the authority of the monarchy, despite the opposition of feudal lords, of Huguenots, and of foreign rulers. "I am resolved," she wrote, "to seek by all possible means to preserve the authority of the king my son in all things, and at the same time to keep the people in peace, unity, and concord, without giving them occasion to stir or to change anything."

To achieve this end Catherine, by skilful diplomacy, organized the government around herself. With the aid of the Bourbon princes, and with the support of Anne of Montmorency, his relatives, the Châtillons, and several other nobles, she checked the ambitions of the Guises and then proceeded to govern France. This was not an easy task, because Catherine, though clever and crafty, was not trained to rule, and furthermore she was confronted by a very difficult situation. On the one side, she encountered the demands of the fanatical Catholics for the general persecution of the Huguenots, while on the other side, certain Huguenots scorned the idea of mere toleration and turned to uprisings and riots. At the same time extravagance and corruption had driven the state to the verge of bankruptcy, the courts refused to function, and rival political groups were about to divide France into two hostile camps. Meanwhile Philip II of Spain, aware of the confusion in France, cast covetous eyes upon her border domains. France was virtually hanging over a political and a religious precipice.

Various expedients were adopted by Catherine in her efforts to save the monarchy and at the same time to maintain her power. At first, by means of diplomacy and intrigue, she attempted to steer a middle course between the religious parties and political factions. She endeavored to do this by balancing the various political and religious groups one against the other. Later she tried to reconcile the antagonistic elements, and was assisted in that policy when she intrusted her government to the liberal-minded chancellor de l'Hôpital, who was one of the early exponents of toleration and of the supremacy of state interests over all religious or factional issues. But the difficulties appeared insoluble. Concessions granted the Huguenots alarmed many sincere Catholics. Anne of Montmorency joined the Guise party in its effort to suppress Protestantism. Meanwhile Catherine and L'Hôpital tried to reconcile the two religious sects by means of conferences between Catholics and Protestants. No settlement, however, was reached. Finally, the Guise faction refused to obey an edict of January, 1562, in which the government granted the Huguenots certain rights. Civil war was imminent.

THE RELIGIOUS WARS

The conflict started on March 1, 1562. It was precipitated by an unfortunate encounter between the soldiers of the duke of Guise and a Huguenot congregation in which three hundred Huguenots were murdered. This was called the massacre of Vassy. The Huguenots, led by the prince of Condé and admiral Coligny, took up arms, achieving some notable successes, especially the capture of Orléans. Elizabeth of England interfered. First she occupied the port of Havre given to her by the Huguenots. Then she sent troops to aid the Huguenots. Several defeats, at Rouen and Dreux, however, convinced the Protestants that they had overestimated their strength. Gladly they accepted the favorable Peace of Amboise (1563), in which Catherine granted liberty of worship under certain restrictions.

The queen mother was not able to restore the damage done by the first civil war. Taking advantage of the religious struggle, bands of robbers and ravishers had put people to ransom and to sack in various parts of France. Destruction of crops caused famine throughout the land.

Having ended the conflict, Catherine turned upon England, forcing the English to leave Havre and to give up claims to Calais for a consideration. After this was achieved, Catherine decided to bring about an era of good feeling in France by means of a tour of the country, taking the court with her. Whatever good impression this might have made on the Huguenots was neutralized by the conference which she held at Bayonne (1565) with Elizabeth, queen of Spain, and the duke of Alva, hated by all Protestants. The Huguenots were certain that plans were being made for an alliance between Spain and France for the purpose of suppressing them. Consequently they felt justified in preparing for war.

The second religious conflict started in 1567. By that time the Catholics were strong enough to secure the fall of the wise exponent of toleration, L'Hôpital, and in the following year they extorted a royal edict unconditionally forbidding the exercise of the reformed cult.

This war marked a slight gain for the Huguenots, who were able to besiege Paris. Their advance, however, was checked by Catholic forces in the bloody and bitterly-contested battle of Saint-Denis (1567). Two years later the Huguenots suffered several defeats, and the jubilant Catholics believed that the enemy would have to submit. They were mistaken, for influential nobles, fearing Spanish and Guise control, joined the Huguenot cause. Furthermore, the Protestant strongholds were no longer in the north, but in the south and in the west. In the ancient provinces of Poitou, Guienne, Gascony, and Languedoc, the people made Protestantism a phase of their particularistic spirit. Here the centralizing tendency which made possible the rise of the absolute monarchy was exceedingly tenuous. Local privileges, instead, were more esteemed and more insisted upon. Consequently the people, especially in the southern cities, who accepted Protestantism, continued their religious and political ambitions, and strove for political rights as well as religious liberty.

By 1572 Catherine was desperate. She had failed in her attempts to satisfy all sects by means of a policy of conciliation. Nor was she successful in her scheme to seduce the rebellious nobles by sending to them beautiful maids of honor, of good rank and of low principles. It is true that Condé fell in love with one of them, forgetting everything else, including wife, party, and religion. But most of the leaders could not be seduced.

Meanwhile Huguenots and Catholics were forming independent political parties. The former attempted to arrange alliances with England and the German states, and also supported the revolt of the Netherlands against Spain. The Catholics, under the stimulus of the Jesuits, conducted an effective propaganda. Catholic Leagues were formed to combat the organizations of the Huguenots, the latter commanded by the energetic and capable admiral Coligny. A crisis was reached when Coligny and his followers induced the court to carry on friendly negotiations with England, and to check Spanish ambitions. The French ultra-Catholic parties and Spain planned at once to oppose the policy and also to stop the growing tendency towards religious toleration on the part of the court.

The brave and resourceful Huguenot admiral undoubtedly exerted considerable influence, especially upon the young Charles IX. Because of this he incurred the hostility of the powerful queen-mother. Determined that no one should usurp her control of the government, she planned to get rid of this rival. Meanwhile Coligny urged Charles to oppose Spain in the Netherlands and to marry his sister, Marguerite of Valois, to the young Protestant ruler, Henry of Navarre. Hearing of these plans and fearing the anger of Philip II of Spain, Catherine decided to act. She and the ultra-Catholics now plotted the assassination of Coligny. This failed. The excitement on both sides was intense. Clearly Catherine and her confederates derived no good from the plot. Panic-stricken at the thought that this crime might be brought home to them, they decided to commit another and far greater. All the Huguenot leaders and their associates must be killed. By doing this, Catherine and the Guises would not only get rid of Coligny and of his followers, who were too powerful at court, but would also win the support of Catholic Spain, in case England intervened.

Charles IX, who was personally on good terms with Coligny, hesitated, when the plot was suggested. But he was too weak a youth to hold out long. Finally, he sent messengers to all quarters with verbal orders to kill the leading Protestants.

Coligny was the first victim of the massacre. Condé and Henry of Navarre escaped by means of a forced conversion to the Catholic faith. Meanwhile, the conspiracy to assassinate Coligny had developed into the unfortunate religious massacre of St. Bartholomew's Day. From August 24th to October 3d, 1572, a wholesale killing took place in almost all of the provinces. Thousands of Huguenots were murdered in this attempt, according to Catherine de' Medici, "to wipe out those subjects who were rebellious to God and to Charles IX."

The massacre failed to achieve this end. Flaming with new anger, the Huguenots throughout France flocked to the standards of their remaining leaders, swore revenge, and called upon all Protestants to come to their assistance. Catherine, the Guises, and their associates regained control of the government only to be confronted by a new outburst of civil war. Dark days were ahead.

The massacre was a colossal blunder. No individual or party really benefited as a result of it, except perhaps those against whom it was directed, the Huguenots. They now received aid from many individuals who previous to the massacre had assumed a hostile attitude. Many moderate Catholics, called *Politiques,* joined forces with them. These men opposed this bloodshed and advocated toleration as the only agency by which the religious question could be settled, peace attained, and the monarchy saved. The pope, Philip II, the Guises, and Catherine, however, believed that the massacre had ended the religious problem. Henceforth France was to be Catholic. And so delighted was Philip II when he heard of the massacre that he "is said to have laughed for the first time in his life."

In France the massacre of St. Bartholomew's Day marked a definite stage in the decline of the French monarchy. Hitherto, the king, advised by the duke of Guise, Montmorency, and other men of high rank, had retained the respect of his people. Both Catholics and Protestants proclaimed their loyalty to him, even though they fought each other. Beginning with the massacre, however, inferior individuals, including a number of "detested foreigners," counseled the king in governmental matters, and many Frenchmen lost confidence in their sovereign. He was now bitterly opposed by thousands of persecuted Huguenots. The right of resistance to the crown was openly discussed in certain quarters, especially among ambitious Catholic and Protestant noblemen, who at last saw a chance to abolish the "despicable despotism" at Paris, and to restore the "legal feudalism" of former days.

These noblemen were not alone in their opposition to the monarch. Many Huguenots of the bourgeois class, influenced by political rights they enjoyed in their local assemblies, joined the nobles in their attacks upon despotism, planning thus to increase their political power. A number of Huguenot writers also attacked the absolute monarchy in their writings. They challenged particularly the doctrine that the king held his power immediately of God, there being no limitations upon it except those he himself would impose. Hotman, in his *Franco-Gallia,* and Duplessis-Mornay, in his *Rights Against Tyrants,* made a plea for constitutional monarchy, but more especially against Roman, Spanish, and Guise influence.

THE "POLITIQUES" SUPPORT THE MONARCHY

At this critical time the third or middle-course party prepared to support the monarchy. These *Politiques,* many of them Catholic noblemen, favored a Gallican or a national church, accepted the divine-right idea, and believed in the Machiavellian conception that the state was an end in itself, superior to all rules of law, natural or civil. As practical men they realized that the religious struggles and the factional rivalries might lead to foreign intervention and the partition of France. This must not occur. Influenced by personal or by patriotic motives they believed that the welfare of the state should supercede all other interests. In other words, they decided that their own advantage required the preservation of the French monarchy. Hence they were determined to defend the government against the attacks of all internal or decentralizing forces. They maintained that the anti-monarchical tendencies of the religious wars had clearly demonstrated the necessity for toleration, if France was to maintain her existence as a consolidated state and to protect herself against the attacks of foreign foes. The religious wars, they said, must end; and, like L'Hôpital, Catherine's great chancellor, they believed that religious toleration alone could stop them.

People living in the sixteenth century disagreed in their estimate of the real significance of the *Politiques*. They were, in the interesting phrase of their enemy, Tavannes, "those who preferred the repose of the kingdom to the salvation of their souls; who would rather that the kingdom remain at peace without God than at war for Him." To a certain extent this was true. The *Politiques* opposed the Catholic League, among other reasons, because the latter interpreted Catholicism as an international religion. They claimed that as true believers of that faith the leaguers could consider union only in terms of a common faith transcending the limitations of patriotism and of nationalism. To the *Politiques* this idea was impractical and inimical to the existence of the state. On the other hand, they believed that the Calvinistic doctrines of the Huguenots caused the latter to display an equally dangerous inclination to favor the political right of the nobility, and thus to encourage the forces leading to decentralization. This must not be allowed. The *Politiques,* therefore, maintained that they alone appreciated the unfortunate results of the political and religious trends of the day, and had the courage to present a practical theory of government which would free the state from its perilous position by forcing all parties to settle their disputes upon considerations of national interests. According to their able political philosopher, John Bodin (1530-1596), they placed the welfare of the state first, and vigorously advocated toleration to end the destructive wars and to strengthen the authority of the king.

The *Politiques* as an organized party became especially powerful in southern France. In this particularistic region the adherents of the two religious creeds were evenly balanced and closely intermingled; consequently the wars were brutal and destructive. Ambitious leaders were now in a position to take advantage of the religious struggles and the absence of royal authority to create semi-independent states. This happened in the province of Languedoc, where the *Politiques* and the Huguenots, in 1574, united under the rule of Henry of Montmorency-Damville. Appointed governor and lieutenant-general of Languedoc by the king in 1563, this forceful member of the Montmorency family in ten years made himself virtually an uncrowned king in the south, collecting taxes, raising armies, and enacting laws.

Damville became an ardent *Politique,* realizing that the continuation of the religious wars would destroy France and ruin him. Because of his power he was soon courted by all factions. Wisely he bided his time, maintaining his authority through his control of the *Politiques* and the Huguenots in the south. Meanwhile he planned to throw his support to the king when that monarch definitely came out in favor of the *Politique* ideas.

The boy kings were unable to furnish the leadership Damville desired. Charles IX, broken in body and haunted by superstitious terrors, was happily relieved of his earthly troubles through his death (1574). Henry III, his brother, succeeded him. Unfortunately Henry III was not "every inch a king." He was, it is true, intelligent, interested in culture, and had many good qualities. But he was his mother's spoilt child. Brought up among the girls Catherine sent to seduce the enemy, "he was in a continual state of nervous and sensual titillation that made him avid of excitement and yet unable to endure it." His life was a continual debauch, "ever seeking new forms of pleasure in unusual ways." For instance, "he had a passion for handsome young men, called 'the darlings,' whom he kept about him dressed as women." Even to the most worldly-minded men of the sixteenth century, Henry III was not altogether normal.

Catherine de' Medici was determined to protect the interests of her favorite son. She governed, while Henry indulged himself. Meanwhile the religious controversy continued, and Catherine found her task increasingly difficult.

THE CATHOLIC LEAGUE TRIES TO CONTROL THE MONARCHY

The ultra-Catholics, finding the crown impotent under the weak Henry III, decided to renew their efforts to control the government. Led by Henry, duke of Guise, they perfected their organization, called the Catholic League, in 1576, bringing in the numerous "local chapters" already established. By means of this organization they planned to restore the complete supremacy of the Roman Catholic faith, and "to restore to the provinces and estates of this kingdom the rights, privileges, franchises and ancient liberties such as they were in the time of King Clovis, the first Christian king." The Leaguers revived the doctrine of sovereignty generally held in the Middle Ages, namely, that the kingship was based on the will of the people. They claimed that the crown at no time had removed all competing or checking agencies by which the people might express their will. In their opinion, the king was not omnipotent. The nobles to a great extent controlled the military forces of the nation; the middle classes filled many legal and administrative offices; while most of the large towns still elected their magistrates and provisioned their garrisons. To these checks on the power of the crown they finally added another one—the vague prerogative of the Estates General.

This platform of the Catholic League was significant. It meant that these Catholic extremists in the north, like the Huguenots in the south, were angling for popular support by promising to those who believed in the reestablishment of ancient feudal rights, the restoration of their privileges. Many middle-class men, favoring the revival of the Estates General, joined the nobles in this attempt to return to the "good old medieval days."

Apparently this program was popular, for membership in the League increased rapidly in 1576. Henry III, who at first had disavowed all part in St. Bartholomew's Day and had given the Huguenots liberty of worship everywhere save in Paris, was now in an embarrassing position. He opposed the threat to his authority in the preëminence accorded the powerful feudal lord, the duke of Guise, as chief of the Catholic party, but he feared even more the great body of public opinion represented in the League. What was he to do? He realized that he could not afford to oppose this organization, so powerful in

Paris. Finally, he decided to eliminate his enemy, the duke of Guise, by recognizing the League and by declaring himself its head. By this act Henry III literally dug his own grave. The Huguenots and the *Politiques*, who opposed the League's religious and political policies, lost confidence in him. Meanwhile the duke of Guise, supported by the great majority of Leaguers, made plans to deprive the king of his authority if not his crown.

Henry III tried to satisfy the demands of the various parties by calling a meeting of the Estates General. This body gathered at Blois in December of 1576 and was dominated by the Leaguers (the *Politiques* and Huguenots refusing to send representatives). Led by the duke of Guise these ultra-Catholics attempted to limit the authority of the king, demanding that Henry III should be bound to turn into law any proposition passed by the three orders. In addition they tried to impose a council of thirty-six advisers upon the crown. Henry evaded the first demand, but yielded to the second.

Henry III decided to obtain the support of the Huguenots before he lost everything. Declaring all leagues abolished he entered into a close alliance with the leader of the Huguenots, Henry of Navarre. In the one thing which would have restored confidence in the monarchy —the ending of the civil wars—he failed. Except for breathing spells, obtained through temporary agreements, the conflicts continued.

By 1584 these wars had virtually bankrupted the government. Meanwhile, the attempts of the king to raise money only increased the poverty of the masses. Every estate and every province was urged to contribute as much as possible, and most of them humbly, but firmly, begged for relief from these ruinous exactions. The only prosperous men seemed to be the government agents and contractors. For the first time in the history of France the people were becoming thoroughly disaffected and some of them semi-republican in feeling.

HENRY OF NAVARRE, NEXT IN LINE FOR THE THRONE

In 1584 occurred an event far more important than the four religious conflicts which followed St. Bartho-mew's Day. This was the death of the duke of Alençon, only remaining brother of Henry III, and heir to the throne of France. Inasmuch as Henry III had no sons, the Huguenot leader, Henry of Navarre, of the Bourbon house, was next in line for the throne.

Having revoked his recantation of the Huguenot religion, made after St. Bartholomew, Henry of Navarre was now head of a powerful Protestant organization in southern France. He realized that he would encounter desperate opposition in his attempts to succeed Henry III. The Guises, the pope, and Philip II of Spain, would do everything in their power to oppose him. Wisely he turned to the *Politiques* for support, arranging an alliance with their leader, Henry of Montmorency-Damville (1585).

Henry of Guise, as head of the Catholics, with the approval of Philip of Spain and of the pope, selected the uncle of Henry of Navarre, Charles, cardinal of Bourbon, a stupid and violent man of sixty-four, as the legal heir to the throne. In January, 1585, a secret compact was agreed upon by the heads of the house of Guise, the Spanish representatives, and the cardinal of Bourbon. The articles included the exclusion from the crown of a heretic, or of anyone who aided the heretics. It also provided for the annihilation of heresy, and for the full acceptance of the decrees of the Council of Trent. As part of the agreement Philip II promised to furnish large subsidies in return for which the cardinal was to grant

Spain certain favors, including a foothold north of the Pyrenees.

The "war of the three Henrys" was inevitable. Leading the Huguenots, Henry of Navarre won his first important victory in the battle of Coutras (1587). Meanwhile Henry of Guise made Henry III virtually a prisoner in Paris. Supported by the citizens of Paris, Guise usurped the authority of the king. Henry III, rather than submit to this treatment, escaped from Paris (1588).

At Blois, where the Estates General was meeting, the king tried to oppose the Guise faction. He soon discovered that the Catholic Leaguers controlled that body. Henry III by now was desperate. He realized that unless he acted quickly he might lose his throne to the duke of Guise. Then he made his last great mistake. By his order, the duke of Guise, popular hero of the people, was murdered. "My, but he is tall," the king is said to have remarked as he kicked the dead body of his rival. "Now I am king," he wrote. He was mistaken. As soon as the news of this assassination reached the Leaguers they declared Henry III deposed and refused to deal with him. Frankly revolutionary, the League exercised its authority in Paris under the leadership of a Council of the Sixteen. "No king of France was ever treated as Henry III was at this time. His authority was virtually extinct."

In January, 1589, Catherine de' Medici passed away, her death hastened by this unfortunate tragedy and by her anticipation of the disastrous consequences to follow. Henry III, the last of the house of Valois, was left to his own resources—very limited at that time. Now he decided to flee to the camp of Henry of Navarre and to arrange an alliance with him. Henry of Navarre welcomed the frightened king. The royal presence gave Navarre an opportunity to bring the Huguenots as well as the *Politiques* to support the monarchy. The Leaguers, not the Huguenots, he claimed, were bent on the destruction of the kingdom. Meanwhile the Protestants, realizing that their leader was heir to the throne, gave up their democratic tendencies, and became loyal monarchists. The Catholic Leaguers, however, continued their assaults upon absolutism.

Henry III was not permitted to participate in the struggle to save royal authority. On August 1, 1589, he was assassinated by a fanatical monk who failed to realize that his deed of vengeance opened to a Huguenot the path to the throne. The dying ruler recognized Henry of Navarre as his heir; the crown of France would now be in the hands of a Huguenot—if he could get it.

Henry IV was one of the most intelligent, vigorous, and able of kings. A dashing soldier, thirty-five years of age, of undaunted personal courage, affable, genial, eloquent, witty, quick of repartee, sincerely interested in the welfare of his country, pleasure-loving and of easy morals, his virtues readily won friends, while his faults were lightly condoned. "In a song still popular, he is called the gallant king who knew how to fight, to make love, and to drink. He is also remembered for his wish that every peasant might have a fowl in his pot." Most important, he was a patriot, determined to subordinate all issues, including the religious problem, to the welfare of the state. Coöperation for the general good constituted his platform. The reëstablishment of the absolute monarchy and the rise of a powerful French state were the results.

The difficulties confronting Henry IV in his attempt to become king in 1589 were enormous. The League refused to consider his claim, and Paris closed its gates upon his approach. Cardinal Bourbon was declared king as "Charles X" and the League, aided by Spanish troops under the duke of Parma, prepared to resist the heretic enemy. But Henry IV took the offensive, and made a determined effort to defeat the enemy and to capture Paris. Winning the battle of Ivry (1590), he proceeded to invest the capital of France.

Henry IV failed to enter Paris. Bravely defended by the citizens led by the Council of the Sixteen, the sister of the duke of Guise, and a cardinal, the city held out until relieved by the duke of Parma and his Spanish troops from the Netherlands. The death of "Charles X," May, 1590, again left the throne without a Catholic claimant. Philip II now tried to secure the crown for his daughter, or for himself, while the duke of Mayenne, leader of the League in place of the duke of Guise, expressed a willingness to accept the title. Meanwhile the Council of the Sixteen, drawn from the councils which directed the sixteen quarters in Paris, urged the candidacy of the son of the late duke of Guise, proposing his marriage with the Spanish infanta.

Henry IV realized that he could not become king by military force alone. Although many moderate Catholics joined the so-called cause of royalty and of legitimism, the great majority refused to support Navarre, because he was a Protestant. Conscious of his legitimate right and fearful of foreign intervention, they really wanted to back him—but they refused to do this as long as he remained a heretic.

At first Henry IV refused to consider the religious opposition. While never an overly-religious man, he wanted to be loyal to his Huguenot followers. But after making a number of fruitless attempts to obtain the throne by force, he admitted that the crown could be gained only by means of his conversion to the Catholic religion. As a *Politique* he found ample justification for this act. In fact he is supposed to have said, "Paris is worth a Mass." At any rate he abjured the Protestant faith in 1593, and was received into the bosom of the Roman Catholic church.

The Huguenots were enraged when they heard of his conversion, while numerous Catholics doubted his sincerity. The *Politiques,* however, rallied to the throne, fearing Spanish control and demanding the end of the civil wars. The conversion of Henry IV weakened the opposition. The League rapidly melted away, enabling Henry IV to be crowned in 1594 and to enter Paris where he received the homage of the Sorbonne and of the *Parlement* of Paris.

HENRY IV, CHIEF OF THE "POLITIQUES"

As king, Henry IV soon justified the support of the *Politiques.* He did this by leading his troops in a national conflict against Philip II of Spain, who, enraged at seeing France escape from his clutches, had declared war in 1595. By 1598, Spain was only too glad to listen to terms of peace. Consequently, in the Peace of Vervins, Henry IV forced Spain to recognize the Pyrenees mountains as the frontier between France and Spain, and to waive all claims in his kingdom. Thus the French king instituted the *Politique* policy to make France, instead of Spain or Austria, the leading power in Europe. Richelieu and Louis XIV completed this plan in the seventeenth century.

Henry IV also justified *Politique* support by ending the civil wars. At the same time he obtained the backing of most Huguenots by issuing the edict of Nantes (1598). By the terms of this edict Henry IV legalized the religious toleration which the Huguenots already possessed.

They were to have the right of practising their religion in two places in every bailiwick, with the exception of Paris and other large towns, and were to be eligible for all offices. Moreover, they were to have a special chamber, called the Edict Chamber, in every *parlement*, in which Huguenots were to be tried. In addition to these concessions, Henry IV also granted them the right to hold synods, subject to certain restrictions, and for eight years they were to control over 200 towns as security for the king's word. This last concession was ill-counseled. It actually created a state within a state. Huguenots in control of these towns were able to build forts and to raise armies for their own defense. The Catholic clergy and the *Parlement* of Paris opposed this edict, but the personal influence of Henry IV was powerful enough to insure its acceptance.

In addition to defeating Spain and ending the civil wars, Henry IV earned the title, Chief of the *Politiques*, by reëstablishing the authority of the monarch. He did this by depriving many turbulent nobles of their political power and by replacing them with men dependent upon and loyal to himself. Moreover, he revived not only the political, but also the economic phases of absolutism. Most of the Valois rulers had planned, as benevolent despots, to stimulate, to encourage, and to support the economic development of France. Foreign wars, domestic troubles, and, in many cases, lack of ability prevented them from doing these things.

Henry IV achieved what the Valois rulers had only planned. In his development of the economic resources of his kingdom he was aided by Sully, an able exponent of Calvinistic thrift and economic enterprise. This stern, gloomy, penurious Huguenot first reformed the collecting of taxes. By reducing expenditures and by decreasing the amount of corruption involved in the collection of the taxes, Sully created a surplus in the treasury.

Sully also believed that land was the source of all wealth. Consequently he did much to promote scientific agriculture and to improve transportation. In southwestern France large swamps were drained, and a system of canals was planned to connect the important rivers. Bridges were built, roads constructed, taxes on farming pursuits lessened, and the nobles were forbidden to hunt where crops were growing. Mulberry trees were brought to central France in order to stimulate the silk industry, which assumed great proportions, especially at Lyons. Today it is still one of the leading industries in France. The manufacture of glassware and pottery was also encouraged by Sully. Colonies were established in the Americas and in Asia.

Henry IV participated in the economic development of France. Encouraging the growth of commerce and of industry, he helped to perpetuate the policies of the great monarchs of the twelfth and thirteenth centuries, to make the middle classes efficient and prosperous. This selfish, yet patriotic and far-seeing ruler did everything in his power to aid his bourgeois allies, believing that their gratitude would enable him to strengthen his authority at the expense of the nobles. Thus fortified, he proceeded to limit the authority of the *parlements* and of his governors in the provinces. Few, indeed, opposed his autocratic tendencies. Contented as a result of the return of prosperity, the people, especially the middle classes, gladly obeyed this genial, capable despot, and willingly gave up their feudal and republican ambitions. Later, the descendants of Henry IV failed to continue his *Politique* policies. The results were a break between the middle classes and king; the revival of democratic ideas slowly and indirectly; and eventually the French Revolution, leading to the fall of the old régime and the rise of the bourgeoisie.

REASONS FOR FAILURE OF PROTESTANTISM TO DOMINATE FRANCE

Protestantism never regained the important position it had held in sixteenth-century France. The conversion of Henry IV and the revival of absolutism marked the failure of the Huguenots to dominate. Henceforth they continued to lose much ground, Richelieu depriving them of their political privileges, and Louis XIV of their religious liberty.

It is not difficult to account for the failure of Protestantism to conquer France. Of fundamental importance was the classical concept of one faith, one king, and one law. Before Protestantism entered France, the king virtually controlled the French Catholic church. After that any assault upon religion constituted an attack upon the state. Moreover, France, surrounded by enemies, was dependent upon unity, in order to maintain her position as one of the leading powers in Europe. Her foreign problems and ambitions required that no decentralizing influence develop within. Finally, France was more interested in the pagan than she was in the Christian Renaissance. Rabelais, Montaigne, and other intellectuals, studied and admired the classics, but neglected, nearly despised, the works of the church fathers. In their minds the social and political ideas of Greece and of Rome were reborn.

The spread of Calvinism in France and the civil wars which followed made one important contribution. The supremacy of the state was frankly recognized. Henceforth patriotic Frenchmen subordinated all issues to its welfare. This *Politique* idea saved France in the sixteenth century, made possible the absolute monarchy of Louis XIV, and gave inspiration to the French Revolution. It has remained dominant to the present time.

Chapter III

CALVINISM, AN INTERNATIONAL RELIGION

Like Roman Catholicism, the Calvinist faith became in the sixteenth and seventeenth centuries an international religion. Established by John Calvin in Geneva it spread rapidly, and soon had followers in western Europe and in the Americas. It had characteristics, however, which limited its expansion. Appealing to subjects rather than to monarchs, it failed to make much headway in those countries where the rulers were supreme. In France, the culmination of absolutism in the reign of Louis XIV marked the end of Protestantism as an independent, flourishing, legal religion.[1] A similar fate was experienced by Calvinism in Italy and in Spain.

CALVINISM IN ITALY AND IN SPAIN

In Italy both Lutheranism and Calvinism at first had energetic disciples. The Italian cities of Ferrara and of Naples were especially important as Protestant centers in the sixteenth century, partly due to the presence of a number of able religious leaders. By 1542 the increase of Protestantism in Italy alarmed the pope. Engrossed by foreign politics, he had until then neglected the local problem. Numerous complaints from the clergy and the friars caused him to order the trial of ecclesiastics accused of favoring Protestantism. In the following year

[1] Protestantism did not legally exist in France from the revocation of the edict of Nantes in 1685 until the granting of complete religious toleration in France during the French Revolution.

the Inquisition was used as a means of ending heresy. As a result of this oppression many Italian Protestants fled to other countries, although most of them were arrested and punished.

Calvinism was introduced into Spain in the sixteenth century through the efforts of two brothers, Alfonso and Juan de Valdés. By 1570, however, it had been practically driven out of this country. Aided by the famous leader, Ignatius Loyola, the Jesuit organization, and the Inquisition, Spain was able not only to extinguish Protestantism, but also to play an important part in the Catholic counter-reformation by which the church checked or obliterated Protestantism in many places.

CALVINISM IN WESTERN GERMANY

By the middle of the sixteenth century it looked as if Calvinism would conquer a large part of central Europe. The elector Frederick III of the Palatinate, who had been a Lutheran, signalized his adhesion to the Genevan doctrine by publishing the Heidelberg Catechism in 1563. As in other Calvinistic communities, the church in the Palatinate was governed by a council of ministers and of laymen, who took special pains to see that such amusements as drinking, dancing, and fortune-telling were abolished. Frederick III found it difficult to maintain his Calvinistic state, encountering the opposition of neighboring Lutheran princes and of his overlord, the Holy Roman emperor. Nevertheless, he died in 1576, "a good man and a sincere Christian," who attempted to "live up to his convictions faithfully, although they were one-sided."

Frederick was a typical Calvinistic ruler. Possessing a cultivated mind, he was deeply interested in education, in establishing primary schools in each village of his state, and in doing much to encourage the growth of the university of Heidelberg. In his life simplicity and economy constituted his two chief aims. Bitterly opposed to those things he considered frivolous, he even went so far as to disregard the fine arts as not worthy of his attention. During his administration no improvements were made in his castle. Dismissing his orchestra, he was forced to borrow musicians from his neighbors when marriage feasts necessitated their presence. Although he gave little time to it, his only amusement was hunting. Devoting most of his life to the business of governing the Palatinate, he left behind him a prosperous and a well-governed state.

During his reign and that of his successor, John Casimir, the Palatinate became the center of Calvinism in central Europe. From it troops were sent to aid the French Huguenots, as well as the Dutch, in their struggles for religious freedom. Participation in the affairs of other countries, however, paved the way for the fall of Calvinism in the Palatinate.

Calvinism entered other states in western Germany during the sixteenth century. In Nassau, Bremen, Hesse, Baden, and Anhalt, this religious sect had many followers. Brandenburg also possessed numerous Calvinists, including the elector, John Sigismund (1608-1619), and his son, George William. Intolerant in their attitude towards Calvinists as well as Catholics, the Lutherans dominated the religious situation, although, after the Thirty Years' War (1618-1648), both Calvinists and Catholics were tolerated.

CALVINISM IN BOHEMIA, POLAND, AND HUNGARY

Calvinism and Lutheranism entered Bohemia in the sixteenth century. Taking advantage of the nationalist movement directed against the overlordship of the Hapsburg emperors, these sects, especially the Calvinists, supported Frederick V of the Palatinate in his attempt to become king of an independent Bohemia. The Holy Roman emperor, exponent of the international Catholic church as well as of the imperial idea, frustrated this design. In 1620 the battle on the White Mountain ended the Protestant and Bohemian "fight for freedom." Frederick V, the Calvinist king, was forced to leave Bohemia, and that country was once more in the hands of the Holy Roman emperor, Ferdinand II. Protestantism, especially Calvinism, was now driven underground and the supremacy of the Catholic religion was reëstablished, mainly by the efforts of the Jesuits.

Protestantism was introduced into Poland, an important outpost of Catholicism, in the sixteenth century. Lutherans, followed by Anabaptists and Calvinists, entered this proud kingdom, affecting the masses as well as the aristocrats. At first the Polish rulers tolerated these new sects. Sigismund II, who ascended the throne in 1548, even professed an interest in their beliefs. Protestantism, however, was doomed in that kingdom, though its adherents were granted religious toleration by an edict of 1573. During the reign of Sigismund III (1587-1632) the failure of Lutherans and Calvinists to coöperate, and the effective work of the Jesuits and other agencies of the Catholic reformation, virtually resulted in the extinction of the various sects.

Curiously, Calvinism made more headway in Hungary than in any other large state in central Europe, with the exception of the Palatinate. Entering this country from Bohemia in 1563, it soon won many converts. Indeed, both Lutheranism and Calvinism steadily spread during the latter half of the sixteenth century, until they had the support of a majority of the inhabitants of this country. By 1586, the Jesuits, again taking advantage of the quarrels between the two Protestant parties, instituted an ardent attack, with such success that, by 1634, the Catholics regained a majority in the Hungarian Diet. Nevertheless, Protestantism has survived with considerable vigor down to recent times, numbering in 1910 about one-fifth of the total population.

CALVINISM'S FAILURE TO DOMINATE WESTERN AND CENTRAL EUROPE

Calvinism failed to become the principal religion in the various states in central Europe and in the Scandinavian peninsula during the sixteenth century. In Sweden, for example, the Lutherans had, by the end of the century, checked a Calvinistic attempt to become the dominant religious group. Several reasons can be given for the Calvinistic non-success in these regions. In the first place, continual controversies between Lutherans and Calvinists, especially over the celebration of the Lord's Supper, made it impossible for the Calvinists to make much headway. Opposed by the Lutherans in their strongholds and repressed by the Holy Roman emperor, who was aided by the Catholic reformation, the Calvinists were either eliminated, or made a distinct minority in this part of Europe.

In the second place, the Calvinists lacked real leadership. Appealing usually to the bourgeois classes rather than to the aristocrats, the Calvinists were not able to win the support of the generals and statesmen, who usually came from the nobility. Lutheranism and Catholicism, on the other hand, supporting firmly the authority of king, emperor, or pope, were able to command that leadership which the Calvinists lacked.

SIGNIFICANCE OF CALVINISM IN CENTRAL EUROPE

The spread of Calvinism in central Europe did contribute noticeably to the establishment of a certain degree of religious toleration. Increasing in numbers and in influence there, they demanded that the Peace of Augsburg (1555), in which equal rights in the Holy Roman Empire were guaranteed to the adherents of the Roman Catholic church and the Lutheran church, should include themselves. In other words, Calvinist rulers, as well as Lutheran and Catholic princes, should determine the religion of their principalities. This status they finally obtained at the conclusion of the Thirty Years' War, due largely to the efforts of the new head of Brandenburg, Frederick William, the "Great Elector" (1640-1688).

By supporting the Calvinist demands, this capable ruler realized that he would promote the interests of his state. Educated in Holland, he had returned to Brandenburg determined that his possessions, Brandenburg and Prussia, should remain no longer a playground for foreign soldiers. Instead, he intended by establishing religious toleration, by centralizing his government, and by favoring economic developments, to make his land a powerful and a prosperous state. His liberal religious policy resulted in the emigration of thousands of Huguenot artisans to Brandenburg-Prussia, especially after the revocation of the edict of Nantes (1685). Moreover, a large number of Calvinistic Dutch farmers were welcomed by the "Great Elector." These energetic foreigners soon justified Frederick William's policy of religious toleration. Playing an important part in the economic development of his state, they did much to prepare the way for the rise of the powerful Prussian kingdom of Frederick the Great (1740-1786).

CALVINISM IN THE NETHERLANDS

In seventeenth-century Holland, the largest province of the Netherlands, Europeans found many economic ideas and customs worth following. Although a small state, lacking fertile soil and threatened by the waves of the sea and by the currents of rivers flowing above surrounding lowlands, it was by that time one of the richest and most powerful of European nations. Wealth encouraged travel, and trading also gave the people in the United Provinces contacts with the outside world. Consequently it is not surprising to learn that they had made much progress in independent political and religious thinking.

As early as the close of the fifteenth century a group of individuals, called the Brethren of the Common Life, were translating the Bible and were encouraging the reading of the Holy Book in various places in the Spanish Netherlands of which the United Provinces were a part. Later in the sixteenth century Lutheranism entered, finding numerous adherents among the lesser nobility and the substantial bourgeoisie, the powerful groups in the Netherlands at that time. Zwingli's views were also accepted by a number of Netherlanders. Calvinism, which came last, appears to have entered the provinces through the French door. In these southern lands, lying close to France, the inhabitants speaking French were easily evangelized by disciples of John Calvin. The first converts were merchants of the great cities, progressive, intelligent, and ambitious people. The poor next embraced the faith. The nobility were little attracted to the disciplinary doctrines of Calvin. During the sixteenth century the teachings of Calvin displaced Lutheranism and Zwinglianism, the reformers becoming Calvinist in doctrine and in discipline.

Calvinism was victorious because it appealed to the dominant middle class. Luther, in breaking from Rome, transferred spiritual authority from the pope to the prince. Consequently the subject's allegiance was not divided between king and pope, but was given entirely to the former. Secular authorities, desirous of ruling over church and state, found it easy to accept Luther's doctrine. The teachings of Calvin, on the other hand, were essentially democratic and republican. Therefore many of his followers enlisted themselves on the side of political liberty and resistance to arbitrary power. It is true that Calvin, himself, recognized the authority of the temporal ruler. In emphasizing the supremacy of God and the right of the representatives of the people to resist a king who disobeyed God's will, however, he encouraged political opposition to tyranny. In the Netherlands, Calvinists sanctioned the struggle to end Spanish control. Their beliefs were accepted by many business men, desirous of obtaining political independence in order to rid themselves of the heavy taxes imposed by Spain, which injured their economic activities. Calvinism also encouraged bourgeois emphasis upon economic pursuits, favoring usury, thrift, and hard work. In the Netherlands it became a middle-class religion.

The Holy Roman emperor, Charles V, and later the Spanish king, Philip II, bitterly opposed the spread of Calvinism in this part of their empire. They realized that the acceptance of this belief would result not only in the expulsion of the Catholic religion, but of Spanish authority as well. To prevent such a catastrophe, Charles V tried to extinguish by edicts and by repressive measures this religious menace, and threatened, at one time, to introduce the Spanish Inquisition. Despite the loss of many liberties and the imposition of heavy taxes by

Charles V the Calvinists retained their beliefs, and still professed loyalty to this genial, popular ruler.

The abdication of Charles V (1556) and the succession of his gloomy and reserved son to the Spanish throne changed the situation. Philip II, wholly Spanish, was determined to save and to control the Catholic church in his empire. To achieve this end he decided to put down the religious rebellion in the Netherlands by enforcing there a complete temporal and spiritual despotism.

His first step was to appoint as his regent in the Netherlands, his half-sister, Margaret of Parma. The opposition to his selection of this outsider, instead of a local leader, was increased when he created a council headed by an ecclesiastic, Granvelle, depriving the local council of state, controlled by local nobles, of most of its powers. The crisis was reached when Philip II widened the scope of the Inquisition and decided to use it throughout the provinces. To enforce his will Spanish troops were sent to the Netherlands. They only served to increase the opposition by plundering and by extorting money from the inhabitants.

Complaints made by the people in the provinces finally caused the regent to order the return of the soldiers to Spain. This concession failed to satisfy the Netherlanders. Convinced that their local charters and privileges were being disregarded, they united in opposition to Philip's representative, Granvelle, forcing the king to recall the cleric in 1564. But the Spanish government refused to withdraw other oppressive measures, including the Inquisition. Angered by this governmental policy, a number of the young nobility, headed by Louis of Nassau, brother of the famous William of Orange, formed an association which they named the League of the Confederates. Their opponents called them "The Beggars."

Expressing opposition to the Inquisition, the League finally decided to put an end to it. Meanwhile the unrest spread to the masses. Rioting occurred and in a fortnight four hundred churches were sacked in Flanders alone.

Impressed by this opposition, the regent promised relief to the Netherlands. Actually Philip II refused to change his policy. Planning to replace Margaret of Parma and to assassinate the leaders of these troublemakers, he sent a new representative, the duke of Alva, to the Netherlands (1567) with strict instructions to put an end to the opposition. Alva lost no time in arresting and in executing two important rebels. Much to his regret he was not able to capture the real prize, the Dutch leader, William of Orange. A reign of terror followed. Assisted by a Spanish "Blood Council," Alva put thousands of persons to death and forced over fifty thousand to leave the country. To pay expenses he then levied unreasonable taxes on the people, causing a financial panic and bringing business to a standstill.

Open revolt now spread throughout the provinces. In 1572 the "Sea Beggars" captured Brielle, a small town on a large island at the mouth of the Meuse river not far from the Hague. Then, with the permission of William of Orange, they terrorized the North Sea, plundering, robbing, and murdering as they went. In possession of Brielle, they also started an advance on land in which the northern part of the Netherlands, including Holland and Zeeland, were wrested from Spain.

In the meantime Requesens replaced Alva in the Netherlands. Wishing to make peace, he held a conference with the rebels at Breda (1575). This was unsuccessful. William of Orange, already acknowledged stadholder of Holland, Zeeland, Gelderland, and Utrecht, demanded religious toleration, restoration of national liberties, and the withdrawal of all foreigners from public service. These conditions the Spanish government refused to accept. War followed.

In the southern provinces the city of Antwerp was sacked by the Spaniards. This caused the people living in that part of the Netherlands, even though they were Catholics, to join the north in opposition to Philip II. All sectional animosities were obliterated and the north and the south, in the Pacification of Ghent (1576), demanded the abolition of the Inquisition, the expulsion of Spanish troops, and the acceptance of William of Orange as governor in Philip's name.

Requesens' death, meanwhile, had resulted in the appointment of Don John of Austria as his successor. Two years later (1578) he was followed by the most capable of Philip's agents, Alexander Farnese, duke of Parma. Taking advantage of the national and religious differences which were causing trouble between the northern and southern provinces, he, by 1585, won back the latter for Philip II. The northern provinces formed the Union of Utrecht for the purpose of defending their civil and religious liberties. This marked the definite separation of the Catholic south from the Protestant north, and the creation of a new Protestant state—the United Netherlands (United Provinces).

The Spanish representative now tried to win William of Orange over. He failed. The assassination of the stadholder in 1584 was the next step in the attempt to end the rebellion in the north. But it was too late. William had virtually completed his work and the future of the United Netherlands was assured. Nevertheless, the passing of this brave and capable man was a distinct loss. "His place in history," says one writer, "is that of a statesman—the father of his country whose death caused little children to weep in the streets." William's second son, Maurice, and his friend, John van Oldenbarneveldt, continued his work.

Lack of a strong central government made it difficult for the northern provinces to organize their opposition to Spain. Under their federal constitution each province retained its own government and its own stadholder. The federal government was supposed, through the States General, to create the defense of the provinces under the captain and admiral general. Feeling the need of a visible head, the states in turn offered the sovereignty to Henry III of France and to Elizabeth of England, both of whom declined.

Elizabeth sent her favorite, the earl of Leicester, to aid the United Netherlands. Meanwhile England and these northern provinces by means of their sea power weakened Spain considerably. In 1588, Philip's great Armada with which he planned to subdue England and the United Netherlands was defeated by the English and a large part of it was destroyed by a storm. Following this, the so-called patriots in the northern provinces, led by Maurice, engaged in a desperate attempt to expel the Spaniards. Between 1591 and 1594 Maurice achieved some remarkable victories. After his death in 1625, his policy was continued by his brother, Frederick Henry, who surpassed Maurice as a statesman, equaled him as a military commander, and won great fame for his skillful siege-operations.

On the seas the Dutch were even more successful than on land. Led by the capable admiral Tromp they constantly harassed the Spaniards. Finally the latter decided to make one determined attempt to destroy Dutch naval supremacy. The largest fleet since the Armada was sent against the Dutch. Arriving in the English channel in September, 1639, the Spaniards were quickly attacked by the Dutch, who virtually destroyed the fleet in a great battle which occurred near the English port of Dover.

This practically ended the struggle between Spain and the United Netherlands. In 1640 the successful revolt of Portugal further enfeebled Spain and the sudden rise of France as a military power alarmed the Dutch. They feared that the Southern Netherlands might pass from weak Spain to strong France. Rather than have this occur, they agreed to peace negotiations which resulted in 1648, in the agreement at Münster, a part of the Treaty of Westphalia, which marked the end of the Thirty Years' War. By this settlement the United Netherlands gained all their demands, the Spanish government recognizing the complete independence of these provinces. The treaty merely legalized a situation which had existed ever since the Spaniards had agreed to a truce with the United Provinces in 1609.

At that time the work of Oldenbarneveldt attracted attention. As pensionary of the province of Holland, he had devoted his energies, ever since the death of William of Orange, to building up a commonwealth. Having achieved this end, he proceeded to secure for his country, Holland, by consummate skill and diplomacy, a place in the councils of Europe out of all proportion to its size.

In 1610, dissension appeared in the United Netherlands. Many citizens, led by Maurice, the military commander and stadholder of the six provinces which comprised the north, favored a strong centralized state. Oldenbarneveldt, however, as leader of the richest and most populous province, Holland, advocated states rights and republicanism. Matters reached a crisis when, in 1613, a national church synod of all Calvinists was called to settle this issue once and for all.

Oldenbarneveldt, despite the fact that the States General in 1617 decided to hold the synod, refused to assent to its summoning. He announced the independence of Holland by ordering the troops to swear allegiance to Holland only, and not to Maurice and to the States General. The nationalist forces, however, were irresistible. Oldenbarneveldt was arrested and executed.

The synod was held at Dort (abbreviation for Dordrecht) in 1618. Although representatives from nearly all Protestant countries were present, the assembly was really a national gathering of Dutch Calvinists. Condemning the Remonstrants (the Calvinists who advocated states rights), they formally announced the supremacy of the central government and called upon the States General to depose or to exile all Remonstrant preachers. At the same time the strict Calvinistic creed, the basis of the Dutch Reformed church, was adopted.

By 1648, the United Netherlands, a small country, was recognized as one of the leading nations in western Europe. Its sailors and merchants had built up a magnificent empire, including the Spice Islands in the East Indies, Guiana in South America, and the Cape of Good Hope in Africa. Moreover, the United Netherlands was experiencing a remarkable outburst of commercial and industrial activity. Amsterdam was the largest seaport in the world, while Haarlem and Leyden possessed thriving industries. Dutch agriculture led in scientific progress; Dutch scientists and mathematicians were unsurpassed anywhere; in the sphere of maritime law the United Netherlands was supreme; and the university of Leyden was one of the leading centers of Protestant learning in Europe. In art the works of Rembrandt and other Dutch painters had few superiors.

At that time, the United Netherlands was one of the few lands of the "free and the brave." From Spain and Portugal came many exiled Jews; from Germany, Calvinists; from France, Huguenots; and from England,

Puritans and Pilgrims. These persecuted people showed their appreciation of the freedom the Dutch offered by furnishing great intellectual leaders, as well as industrious workers. Spinoza and Descartes, the philosophers, for example, found in Holland freedom to express ideas which in other countries would have been suppressed.

The Dutch failed to contribute much along political lines. Perhaps this explains the decline of their state later on. In peace times the seven provinces were styled "free and independent states," forming a loose union of semi-sovereign provinces, bound together by war against Spain. In periods of political tranquillity these provinces refused to coöperate, opposing a strong centralized government. In theory the provinces were ruled by a stadholder, who at first had little executive power, being chiefly a military leader and a servant and official of the States General, which consisted of representatives of the provincial estates. To complicate matters, the advocate or the pensionary of the largest province, Holland, possessed much influence. This all served to prevent the rise of a strong, unified government until the time of William III of Orange (1672-1702). He was powerful enough personally to become virtually an absolute king.

The independent bourgeois and Calvinist Dutch citizens were largely responsible for the opposition to a strong central government. At the same time their desire for political freedom and religious liberty made them the real leaders in the struggle to overthrow Spanish control. To that extent the United Netherlands owes a great debt to Calvin and his beliefs. On the other hand, Calvinism and Protestantism as a whole are indebted to the Dutch. "If it had not been for Dutch money and naval prestige, the Protestants would have probably been completely defeated in the Holy Roman empire." Moreover, the United Netherlands was one of the few countries in Europe where the Catholic reformation failed. This made the Dutch Republic in the seventeenth century the stronghold of Protestantism in Europe.

CALVINISM IN SCOTLAND

Calvinism probably made its outstanding contributions in the English-speaking world, especially in Scotland, in England, and in the Americas. Historians emphasize its importance in Scotland, where an economic revolution accompanied its rise. At the opening of the sixteenth century that country was a backward nation, intellectually, politically, and economically. Her scholars were few, her kings were weak, her soil was poor, and she lacked important commerce or industries. The Catholic church possessed half of the wealth of the country, which the higher clergy and many sons and daughters of noblemen enjoyed as benefices. Moreover, the right of the church to enforce payment of heavy tithes was exercised, causing the clergy and the people to live in a continual state of antagonism.

The relations between the clergy and the nobility were not friendly, inasmuch as the former supported the crown against the nobility. The foreign policy of Scotland was also influenced by this situation. The monarchy favored a French alliance; while the peasants and the nobility, especially when Protestantism entered Scotland, turned to England for support. Conditions in Scotland, indeed, favored a religious revolt.

When Lutheranism first entered Scotland, it encountered unrelenting governmental opposition. Strangers were forbidden to bring Lutheran books into Scotland, and, in 1527, those who insisted upon spreading the new belief were imprisoned. Finally, in 1543, the government virtually admitted that it had failed to check Lutheranism. Heresy was spreading rapidly throughout the land.

About this time the religious situation was definitely affected by politics. Henry VIII, desirous of uniting England and Scotland, proposed that his son marry the daughter of James V of Scotland. A pro-English party with Protestant leanings now appeared in Scotland. This organization was instrumental in bringing about a marriage treaty in 1543. Opposition developed. Led by cardinal Beaton, a pro-French and pro-Catholic group succeeded in abrogating this agreement and in renewing the alliance with France. Civil war between Protestants and Catholics followed, accompanied by a revival of the struggle between England and France. In 1546, cardinal Beaton was murdered, and in the following year the Scottish parliament, controlled by the Catholics, sanctioned the proposed marriage of the infant princess, Mary, queen of Scots, and the dauphin of France, later Francis II.

The Scottish people soon resented the presence of French soldiers in their country, especially when French advisers urged increased taxes for national defense. Meanwhile the emigration of many Protestants from England, especially the arrival of the able Calvinist leader, John Knox, in 1555, revived Protestantism in Scotland.

Knox was a shrewd Scotsman and a sincere Calvinist. Like Calvin he was educated for the Roman Catholic church. But God spoke to him, he claimed, through another heretic, Wishart, and Knox became a reformer, publicly denouncing the church. Arrested because of his fiery words, he was, in 1547, a French galley slave. Two years later he was released and returned to England, where he preached the word of God. Upon the accession of Catholic Mary Tudor to the throne (1553), however, he wisely moved to the continent, where he preached and studied. Spending considerable time in Geneva, "he thoroughly assimilated the principles of the *Institutes,*" which armed him with a mastery of language, argument, scriptural proof, and systematic invective.

In 1555 he returned to Scotland, an organizer, not a mere preacher. Scotland, at that time, was not ready for a new religion. Summoned by the ecclesiastical court in 1556, Knox fled to Geneva. In his absence his effigy was burned.

Heresy continued to grow in Scotland. In 1557 a group of "gentlemen of means" signed a formal document and became known as "The Lords of the Congregation." In this agreement they vowed to risk their lives against "the congregation of Satan" and "to establish the most blessed word of God and of His Congregation." Knox, now urged to return to Scotland, accepted the invitation, and arrived in 1559, determined to organize a Calvinist church.

The government of Scotland was in the hands of the queen dowager, Mary of Guise. She favored France and was instrumental in bringing about the wedding between her daughter, the queen of Scots, and the French dauphin. They were then only fifteen years of age. By treaty, she also virtually deeded Scotland to the king of France, meanwhile trying to check the spread of Calvinism by prohibiting preaching by reformers.

The Lords of the Congregation begged her to cease these oppressive acts, declaring that her commands must be disobeyed, if contrary to God's. She refused. Consequently the basis of resistance to constituted authority was laid. Taking advantage of this situation, Knox proceeded to stir up religious feeling by uttering vehement blasts against idolatry. Riots occurred, churches and monasteries were destroyed, and priests, monks, and nuns were forced to flee.

The Calvinists were not fighting Catholics alone; they

were also striving, they said, to deliver Scotland from French control. Hence they were in a strong position, for patriotism and religious enthusiasm constitute a combination difficult to overcome. Moreover, the Scotch Calvinists had England as a natural ally. Opposing French influence in Scotland, and fearing Catholic supremacy in England and in Europe if Protestantism was conquered in Scotland, Elizabeth of England, much as she disliked Calvin and his ideas, decided to aid the Scotch Lords of the Congregation.

With this help the Scotch gentlemen were victorious. Posing as patriots rather than as rebels, they deposed Mary of Guise in 1559, in order to prevent French control. By 1560 French dominance was ended. Both Scotch and English troops were then able to turn on the Catholics.

Meanwhile Parliament, controlled by the reformers, appointed Knox and five colleagues to formulate the new ecclesiastical policy in *The Confession of Faith*—a compendium of Calvinistic theology. This was ratified by an overwhelming majority of the Parliament of Scotland. Three acts were now passed destroying the old church and abolishing the authority of the pope. All doctrines and practices contrary to *The Confession of Faith* were condemned. Mass was forbidden within the borders of Scotland. Confiscation, exile, and death were the degrees of punishment inflicted upon those who said mass. In other words, the Calvinists were just as intolerant as their opponents, the Catholics.

Knox next provided the church with a constitution by drawing up his *First Book of Discipline.* This was adopted by the church and supplied a scheme for a national church government, a national system of education, and a national system of relief for the poor. Parliament, however, refused to accept it, largely because the

Book of Discipline proposed to nationalize church property and to devote it to the support of the church and of education. Inasmuch as many nobles in Parliament enjoyed incomes from church property, they did not propose to accept a scheme which would force them to disgorge the church lands. Nevertheless, the typical Calvinist theology, outlined in this religious constitution, was adopted, and the church was ruled by preachers and by elders, in various ecclesiastical courts, parish sessions, provincial synods, and a general assembly. In power, these Calvinists now proposed to make Scotland a land of moralists by maintaining a strict discipline through their chief weapon—excommunication.

The most important contribution of the *Book of Discipline* was the projected system of national education. Calvin, Luther, Loyola, all stressed this important activity. But the Scotch reformers, led by Knox, made one outstanding contribution, and that was the conception of education as a national requirement. To them it was not a privilege, but a common need of all. Knox believed that man must be able to read in order to study the Bible and be of the elect by obeying the word of God. Hence rich and poor must be educated. The rich need no compulsion, said Knox. But the poor must be compelled to attend schools, even though the public has to support them.

In this *Book of Discipline* the principles of Christian socialism were embodied. The individual was merged in society, being educated by the church, at the expense of the state, if necessary. His career was selected for him, and his activities and opinions were formed and guided according to the creed and to the discipline set forth by the church. The parish was the unit of society. Through its discipline it prevented excessive luxury and absolute need and, at the same time, it subjected every Scotsman to a moral and to an intellectual discipline such as no other country succeeded in giving its people.

The return of queen Mary from France in 1561 delayed the triumph of the Calvinists. At first she demanded religious freedom for herself as a queen. As the next heir to Elizabeth of England she then waited for the death of the reigning queen or a Catholic rebellion to make her ruler of England. Growing impatient, she "compromised herself in the Catholic plots and risings of Catholic southerners."

Other mistakes and misfortunes, especially her marital troubles, paved the way for her fall. By June, 1567, Mary was virtually a prisoner in the hands of the great nobles of Scotland. The captive queen now was forced to abdicate in favor of her infant son, James VI, who later became James I of England. Meanwhile a regency was selected to rule Scotland. The abdication of Mary signified the triumph of Calvinism in Scotland. *The Confession of Faith* was accepted and the acts against Romanism were passed by Parliament. Among these was the proviso that the sovereign in the future must be a Protestant.

The religious revolt in Scotland had resulted in the creation of a Calvinist church whose members were fierce warriors against their enemies. After the death of Knox (1572) the chief controversy centered around the relationship between the monarch and the church. The rulers favored the episcopal form of church government, rather than the Presbyterian. According to the latter organization the state was the servant of the church. But the king intended through control of the bishop to make that institution a part of the state. This bitter struggle continued throughout the seventeenth century. By 1689, however, the predominance of Presbyterianism in Scotland was assured. At that time a Convention

Parliament adopted a Claim of Right and offered the sovereignty of Scotland to William and Mary. Later a new Parliament abolished the episcopacy in Scotland on the basis that it was "contrary to the inclination of the people."

Presbyterianism was supreme in Scotland. The character of the Kirk, as the Presbyterian church was called,

> was that of a democratic, puritanical democracy. The real rulers of it, and through it of the state, were the ministers and elders elected by the people. The democracy in the Kirk consisted in the rise of most of these men from the lower ranks of the people; its theocracy in the claim of these men, once established in Moses' seat, to interpret the commands of God.

The economic significance of Calvinism was especially apparent in Scotland. The Scotch Presbyterians gladly accepted Calvin's conception of existence as a post of duty which man, like a soldier, must not abandon, but must endure by the grace of God, come what might. It was in accord with the hard necessities and narrow scope of their daily lives. They also concluded that no employment was sordid or mean if respected in the eyes of God. Sanctity to them became attached to property and to work, and reproach to poverty and to idleness. By his conduct alone "the elect," they believed, could glorify God. He was therefore urged to the full development of his God-given powers.

These ideas accompanied and perhaps caused a revolution in economic as well as religious life in Scotland. Objects of former veneration were converted into cash and cannon. Sumptuary laws against extravagance in dress and in food were passed. The nation made forward strides in material well-being. Feudalism disappeared, industry was stimulated, and a powerful middle class arose. Political and economic power passed from the nobles to the people. Meanwhile devotion to worldly callings resulted in efficiency in business and in a passion for gain.

Calvinism also influenced the development of political theories in Scotland. Knox in his sermons and writings introduced democratic ideas. In his opinion, the common man "is called by God regardless of wealth or of learning." The "elect" can not only interpret the scriptures, but also is competent to judge in political affairs. Therefore, the common man, who is of the elect, should govern. This was accepted as the fundamental political belief of the Scots. The supremacy of the General Assembly in Scotland was the actual result. Knox also evolved the concept of deposition. "God's law," he claimed, "exempts from punishment neither ruler nor people," and men may "depose and punish the ruler whom they have inadvisedly elected."

Calvinism in Scotland brought about important social and intellectual consequences. Emulating Calvin, Knox devoted his life to the task of bringing moral order into the habits of the people. He attempted to make Edinburgh a model city, by trying to expel undesirables and to eradicate vice. Laws were enacted regulating conduct on holy days, and controlling markets, amusements, and the printing of books.

Calvinism created a new intellectualism in Scotland. Men had to read the Bible in order to obey the word of God and to be of the elect. In a way this "called men to independent thought and action." Moreover, the need of reading the Holy Book to obtain salvation provoked the habit of inquiry which, according to some writers, constitutes the basis of the fundamental contribution of Scotch Calvinism—individualism. Calvin, they claim, taught men to bring everything to the bar of reason.

The Scots, in assimilating the dogma of the Calvinist church, acquired beliefs and methods of thought which solved knotty problems in theology, in politics, in trade, and in natural science.

Calvinism in Scotland was stern. It was also materialistic and realistic. As such it perhaps helped to rob Scotland of many of the artistic benefits of the Renaissance. Religion was severed from painting and sculpture. Architecture, also, was reduced to a minimum. Imaginative literature, prose, and poetry for a long time were unacceptable, unless based on the scriptures. In fact, Calvinism in Scotland, by disregarding imagination, produced virtually nothing in the fine arts. The Puritans in England and in America to a lesser degree than the Scots, followed the same path. Determined "to chase all blandishments not only from church but from life," they considered art a bit immoral.

CALVINISM IN ENGLAND

In England, king and parliament had attempted, before the religious revolt, to curb the power of the church and to increase governmental authority in religious matters. At the end of the fifteenth century a group of distinguished scholars in England had insisted on a reform of abuses within the church, although they did not declare in favor of a break with the Roman Catholic organization. Nevertheless, the tendency in England as in France was to attain a degree of independence of the papacy, to improve conditions in the church, and to give the people a better opportunity to develop a personal religion. Leaders, called the "Oxford Reformers," earnestly outlined religious and intellectual changes which, in their opinion, would achieve this end.

Political and personal considerations finally led to a

religious revolt in England. Henry VIII (1509-1547) belonged to the house of Tudor which from the beginning of its rule (1485) until its end (1603) maintained one policy—the establishment of absolute power for the crown. His personal desire to get rid of his wife and to marry the attractive Anne Boleyn led to the break from Rome and the creation of the national or Anglican church.

The break encouraged the introduction of Protestantism into England, even though Henry VIII and his followers disliked this movement in all of its forms. Calvinism was particularly opposed. This was partly due to the emphasis by the Calvinists upon predestination. To the Anglicans this doctrine was very obnoxious. The idea the Anglicans hated most of all was the emphasis upon the certainty of salvation of the elect through strict discipline, church organization, and the subordination of the authority of the state to that of the church. To Henry VIII, Calvinism meant the substitution of a local, all-powerful church for the control of the pope. This must not occur. He intended to rule over church and state. Neither the pope nor Calvin should limit his authority. Instead, a national or Anglican church should bow to the royal prerogative.

Calvinism seeped into England, especially during the latter half of the sixteenth century. At that time "the name 'Puritan' was given to the Calvinist by his enemy, at first a mocking designation." Opposition, however, failed to check the spread of this religious organization. Favoring economic progress, it appealed to the middle classes who did not consider poverty a virtue. Moreover, England was a growing commercial nation; consequently Calvinist support of capital and credit was especially welcome. According to one writer, "such teaching, whatever its theological merits or defects, was admirably designed to liberate economic energies, and to weld into a disciplined social force the rising *bourgeoisie*." [2]

When Elizabeth became queen (1558), Calvinism was gaining ground rapidly, especially at Oxford university. While she tolerated the various religious sects, especially the Catholics and the Puritans, she planned, at the same time, to rebuild the Anglican church and to make it the great national denomination of all Englishmen. Under this freedom, Calvinism continued to spread. In 1570 it was so popular that the pope, in his excommunication of Elizabeth, accused her of "celebrating the impious mysteries of Calvinism." This was not true. Elizabeth was interested in her political career, not in religious matters.

Attempts were made to "purify" the Anglican church to satisfy the Puritans. But the reforms in ritual were not satisfactory. The Puritans wanted not only the break with the pope, but also a drastic abolition of Catholic dogmas and ceremonies. Lacking governmental support, their influence would have been slight, if their ideas had not appealed to the commercial classes. Attacking the socially frivolous nobility, the Puritans obtained the backing of the traders, especially when they glorified "hard work" and the accumulation of wealth as well as the salvation of the soul.

In 1603, Elizabeth was followed by her cousin, James VI of Scotland. In England he was known as James I. Catholics and Puritans now begged to have their beliefs recognized, and James I decided to give them a hearing. In the meeting at Hampton Court (1604) the Puritans first presented their cause. Dr. Reynolds, their leader, in the course of the discussion, unfortunately suggested that certain theological disputes be referred for settlement to the bishops and to the presbyters. Whereupon

[2] Tawney, *Religion and the Rise of Capitalism,* 111.

James I, without waiting to see what other cards the Puritans had to play, laid his own on the table by announcing that the Puritans must conform to the established or Anglican church, or leave the kingdom. The result was the Pilgrim expedition to New England, in 1620, and the establishment "on this holy ground where the breaking waves dashed high" of the first Calvinist settlement. By this time a group of Calvinists in England, called Separatists, advocated the establishment of an independent church, claiming that the Puritan attempt to purify the Anglican organization was futile.

Charles I (1625-1649), the successor of the autocratic James I, continued the policy of conformity, trying to require the stubborn Scotch Presbyterians to adopt the new English prayer book of 1637. Trouble resulted. In a Scotch church where the Anglican prayer book was read a woman arose in the audience and threw her stool straight at the head of the minister. After this demonstration the audience left the church. The "Bishop's War" (1639-1640) followed, during which a Scotch army invaded England. Confronted by many problems, King Charles I hastened to end the menace by giving the Scotch Presbyterians "peace money."

Meanwhile the foolish ruler decided to punish certain English Calvinists, who, he claimed, had invited the Scotch army into England. This helped to provoke a civil war between the king, backed by the aristocratic Anglicans, and Parliament, controlled by bourgeois Puritans. The latter concluded that the time had now come not only to settle the religious dispute, but also to end the long quarrel between royal prerogative and parliamentary rule.

The conflict started in 1642. In 1643 the parliamentarians made a secret treaty with the Scotch Presbyterians, called the "Solemn League and Covenant," agreeing, in return for military assistance, to introduce uniformity of religion in England, in Scotland, and in Ireland, "according to the example of the best reformed (Presbyterian) churches." The result was defeat for the king (1644), and an attempt to overthrow Anglicanism, as well as the extreme forms of Puritanism. For a short while the Presbyterians controlled Parliament. They convoked a church assembly which drew up the Westminster Confession, ordered the abolition of episcopacy in the whole of England, and prohibited the use of the prayer book in church services.

The substitution of Presbyterianism for Anglicanism failed to solve the religious problem. The majority of soldiers who had opposed the king soon discovered that this dominant Calvinist sect was just as intolerant as the Anglican organization. As independents they opposed the victorious Presbyterians, as well as the moderate Puritans who merely wanted to purify the church of England. These independents opposed episcopacy, the papacy, and the presbyters. They desired complete religious toleration and the right to establish their own churches in their own particular way.

The leader of this group was Oliver Cromwell, a representative in the House of Commons from Cambridge. Cromwell had fought against the king in 1644. He had organized a cavalry regiment, consisting of "honest, sober Christians." Entering battle singing psalms, his troops fought in a prayerful, though highly successful manner. Indeed they might well have been called the "rough riders," inasmuch as they rode "rough" and they rode well. Led by Cromwell, these "Roundheads" played an important part in the defeat of the king's forces.

In a short time a large part of the parliamentary forces were patterned after Cromwell's regiment. The reorganized army was then named the "New Model Army."

Its aim was to end the intolerance of Presbyterianism. "Brethren," Cromwell said one day to his soldiers, "in things of the mind we look for no compulsion but that of light and reason."

Led by Cromwell, the independents were able to put an end to Presbyterian governmental supremacy in 1648, and to behead the king in January of the following year. A commonwealth was now created. England was to have no king, nor house of lords. Instead, the country was ruled by 60 men who had retained their seats in the house of commons. Calling themselves "the representatives of the people," they created in 1653 a dictatorship, the Protectorate, which lasted until 1660.

Cromwell discovered that in order to carry out his ideas and to make England a puritanical and an economic Utopia, he would need to become a dictator. As such he tried to rule England, to conquer Ireland, and to destroy Dutch commerce by means of the Navigation Acts. He planned a moral and a spiritual kingdom of God, perhaps superior to the one at Geneva. He did facilitate in England, through his administration, the rise of a prosperous commercial nation and a prosperous middle class. Strenuous toil, thrift, patience, sober thinking, frequent prayers, and ardent warfare, always on the side of right, Cromwell believed, would result in the establishment of a powerful and of a perfect political, social, and religious order. He stated that this would replace a system which, on account of its corruption and its emphasis upon pleasure, rather than upon self-denial, was doomed.

Cromwell and his followers felt perfectly justified in overthrowing the old régime, and in beheading the king. In their opinion the individual was responsible directly to God. If monarchs failed to rule justly, it was the duty of the elect to put an end to the offending government so that the kingdom of Christ might be set up. Once in power Cromwell's theory of government did not differ a great deal from that of James I. James asserted that "The King is from God, the laws are from the King." Cromwell, as a true Puritan, believed that he was a chosen vessel in God's hand, and that God had placed him at the head of the state. Therefore he ruled as a dictator.

The Calvinists failed to establish a unified church. Instead, they disintegrated. The Presbyterians still advocated a church governed by an association of ministers and laymen, called presbyters. Another group, the Congregationalists, outlined a form of congregationalism, in which individual churches should be established, each independent of the others and free from state interference. There were other forms of Calvinism, including the Independents who opposed any compulsion in matters of faith.

Calvinism, as interpreted by Cromwell, soon bore heavily upon the masses. Its sternness grew tiresome. Many individuals, before long, wanted to be happy as well as prosperous. Certain persons now began to talk of the "good old days." Once in power, Cromwell was too strong to be overthrown. His death (1658) paved the way for the restoration of the monarchy. The Convention Parliament, elected by the people in 1660, recalled Charles II, eldest son of the executed Charles I.

A religious reaction followed. In the first place, Anglicanism was restored and a number of leading Puritans were executed out of respect for the new king. A series of acts were then passed against Catholics and Dissenters—those Protestants who were not Anglicans. Conformity to the Church of England was required.

The death of Charles II (1685) and the accession of James II, his brother, led to another crisis. James was a Catholic. Therefore, he decided to have all laws directed against Catholics, as well as Dissenters, removed. This did not please the Anglicans. Protestants as a whole feared the restoration of Catholicism. The crisis was reached in 1688 when a son was born to Mary of Modena, Catholic wife of James II. Parliament now asked James to descend from his throne, and to permit his Protestant daughter, Mary, and her husband, William of Orange, to take his place. The king opposed this suggestion. Nevertheless, the invitation was sent to William of Orange, who accepted the offer, and soon landed in England with fifteen thousand soldiers. Meanwhile James II, realizing the futility of resistance, fled with his family to France.

This so-called "Glorious Revolution" marked the triumph of Protestantism in England. All Protestants were to enjoy religious toleration, although Dissenters as well as Catholics were denied many political rights until the nineteenth century. Moreover, the rulers of England in the future were to be Protestants and were to sign a statement to that effect.

The outstanding contribution of the "Glorious Revolution," was in the realm of politics. Henceforth the right of Parliament to depose and to appoint the rulers of England was recognized. The king no longer could say that he governed by divine right.

Calvinism played an important part in the evolution of English political ideas. As interpreted by his English disciples, Calvin was a friend of the people, and taught that all governments were based upon "contract, natural rights, fundamental law, and the sovereignty of the people." Whenever a government failed to live up to these obligations, it was the duty of the elect to abolish it and to create a new one more acceptable "as the Kingdom of Christ." "This was to be done," said the English Calvinists, "in a legal way," but revolution, to them, was not illegal when used as a means to an end.

These popular rights found expression in the works of Milton. He justified the Scottish leaders for the deposition of Mary, queen of Scots. These rights were stated in the Solemn League and Covenant, promulgated at the opening of the Civil War between Charles I and Parliament. Moreover, the contract theory, expounded by Cromwell and others in the seventeenth century, made this revolt possible, and also the "Glorious Revolution" of 1688, which, according to many writers, prepared the way for "the rule of the people." "Calvinists" held that "Kings are of the same dough as others. . . . People were not made for Kings, Kings were made for the people." Therefore, the admirers of Calvinism maintained that it was largely responsible for popular rule.

It is difficult to determine the exact political influence of Calvinism in England. It is true that the doctrine of mutual contract between ruler and subject as expressed by leading Calvinists found a notable exponent in England in the person of John Locke (1632-1704), the famous English philosopher. In his works, he aided and justified the resistance to the alleged tyranny of James II, although the same idea had been expressed by many Calvinists before he popularized it.

Calvinism also exerted marked economic influence in England. During the sixteenth and seventeenth centuries that country prospered as the result of the Commercial Revolution. Consequently, any religious belief which sanctioned and encouraged economic enterprise was welcomed by the rising middle classes. Calvinism did this. Its disciples recognized the virtues of commercialism. Capital, credit, banking, usury, and many other economic practices and institutions, were regarded by them as heaven blessed—that is, if they were used in the right way. "No one," they said, "should be vain, because of his wealth." Moreover, wealth should not be used in a sinful way.

The energetic Calvinists prospered in the seventeenth century. "In Lancashire," writes Tawney, "the clothing towns—'the Genevas of Lancashire'—rose like Puritan islands from the surrounding sea of Roman Catholicism."[3] It is not surprising that Calvinism appealed to many middle-class Englishmen. Demanding freedom of economic opportunity, they willingly accepted Calvin's doctrine of personal worth, of self-respect, of self-reliance, and of individual effort.

Adam Smith interpreted in an economic way the fundamental belief of English and Scotch Calvinists—individualism—when he emphasized in his *Wealth of Nations* (1776) the idea that the individual was to be allowed to work out his own salvation in economic affairs, unhampered by governmental restrictions. Just as Calvin and Luther questioned the need of priests in the matter of religious salvation, so Smith opposed governmental interference in the attempts of individuals to attain economic bliss.

His book might well be called the Anglo-Saxon middle-class Bible. Acceptance of its ideas in England signified the end of the old régime and the supremacy of the middle classes. Fussy noblemen, Catholic and Anglican, were doomed as soon as the doctrine of individualism was adopted. Living in castles whose windows had long been stuffed with hay, they stubbornly resisted the assaults of the enemy. But the latter could not be stopped. By the middle of the nineteenth century the English capitalists were in the saddle. Most of these "self-made men" were Calvinists.

Calvinism was not responsible for the ascent of busi-

[3] Tawney, *Religion and the Rise of Capitalism,* 204.

ness men. Many factors contributed to the rise of England as a great commercial and industrial nation. Of these the Technological Revolution was especially important. Nevertheless, Calvinism furnished the religious sanction, valuable at a time when the landowners were in power and the business classes wielded little influence. Favoring honest toil from Monday morning to Saturday night, the accumulation of riches, and the wise expenditure of money for education, social betterment, and religion, Calvinism advocated the chief bourgeois ideas of today.

Finally, Calvinism in England led to the establishment of numerous religious sects. The Quakers, the Methodists, as well as the Presbyterians and the Congregationalists, were greatly influenced by the doctrines and practices of the followers of the French reformer. At the present time, many denominations still show the impress of his ideas.

CALVINISM IN THE NEW WORLD

The part played by Calvinism in the establishment of western civilization in the New World constitutes, to Americans at least, the most important phase of this subject. The first group of Calvinists who came to the Americas were the Huguenots. Settling in a French colony near the city of Rio de Janeiro in Brazil (1555), they soon discovered that they were not wanted, and left. In 1562 a Huguenot settlement was made at Port Royal in the Carolinas. This also failed. Another attempt was made in 1564 to found a Huguenot colony, but this settlement was destroyed by the Spaniards. Nevertheless, when the Carolinas were taken by the English later on, many Huguenots were living in that region.

The Huguenots were unsuccessful in their attempts to

establish themselves in Canada. A small colony was begun near the mouth of the St. Lawrence river in 1599. It failed. A few years later a settlement was made at Port Royal (1603) and then at Nova Scotia. After the death of Henry IV of France, protector of the Huguenots, New France was lost to these Calvinists, the Jesuits obtaining control. Under the auspices of the Dutch government, some Dutch Calvinists and a few Huguenots settled on Manhattan Island in 1623. Part of this group went up the Hudson river and founded the city of Albany. As a group, the Huguenots exerted little influence upon America, although some of our leading business men, at the present time, trace their ancestry back to these early Huguenots who left France in order to enjoy religious freedom.

The English followers of Calvin, the Pilgrims or Separatists, and the Puritans, however, were the people who did more than any other individuals to shape the early political and social history of this country. Establishing settlements at Plymouth, Massachusetts Bay, and in other colonies along the Atlantic, they laid a large part of the foundation upon which was to rest the Thirteen Colonies and later the United States of America. The settlements at Plymouth and Massachusetts Bay illustrate very well the political and social significance of their work.

In the early seventeenth century a group of English Separatists, called Pilgrims, left England on account of religious persecution and settled in Holland. Finding the road to economic success blocked there unless they should become Dutch citizens, join the Dutch Reformed church, and use the Dutch language, these brave people, rather than lose their identity as Englishmen, left Holland. Some returned to England, but most of them decided to emigrate to America. Accordingly they made arrangements with the British Virginia Company for a grand of land, and, in 1620, sailed from England in the *Mayflower* and landed in America at a place they called Plymouth.

There they founded a typical Calvinistic state. A governor was elected annually by church members only. The first executive, Bradford by name, performed not only executive but judicial duties as well. He was all-powerful, except that there was a general assembly to which he went for advice or assistance. In other words, the church members, the elect, had their assembly and chose their governor, who wielded his authority by the grace of God and of the faithful. Only church members could participate in the government. Democracy, as we understand it, certainly did not exist in the early colony.

Church members not only controlled the government, but also the economic life of the community. The leaders of the colony, ten or fifteen men, had the best land and most of the cattle; the second group, the rest of the churchmen, received the remaining good land; while the third group, the potential church members, obtained the land that was left. The fourth group, temporary residents, servants, children, and slaves, received no land, and enjoyed few rights. The colony was run for the benefit of the church members.

Perhaps the most important contribution of the Pilgrims was social. The important teaching in their religion was the practice in daily life of the truth as they believed God revealed it to them in the Bible. Social life at Plymouth consequently constituted an attempt to live in accord with the scriptures. Each day must be filled to its best advantage, because that opportunity would never come again. To see that this was done the leaders took it upon themselves to watch the others carefully. There was no occupation which the community enjoyed more than that of spying, and no duty apparently gave them more pleasure than that of complaining of the conduct of some individual.

Numerous rules and regulations also directed the lives of these sturdy Calvinists. Compulsory attendance at long church services, laws regulating courtships and marriages, were all considered as Calvin conceived them, as means by which a strict morality could be maintained in the community, thus assuring salvation.

The Pilgrim colony at Plymouth was followed by a Puritan settlement at Massachusetts Bay. Inspired by the success of the Pilgrims, a number of energetic middle-class Puritans, unlike the Pilgrims, men of wealth, decided to leave England, believing that they could establish a prosperous economic community as well as a kingdom of God in the Americas. As Puritans, simply favoring a purification of the Anglican church, they were not as radical as their Pilgrim brothers. Nevertheless, they had been oppressed as non-conformists by the Anglican monarchy, and a group of these wealthy Calvinist merchants obtained a grant of land which included a large part of Massachusetts.

In 1628 they established a colony under the governorship of John Endicott. Originally this settlement was a colony ruled from London by a corporation, which had received a charter from the king allowing the company to elect officers and to make laws, provided that they were not contrary to the laws of England. In 1629, however, the company decided to move the government of the colony from England to America. There it was placed in the hands of a governor, a deputy, and eighteen assistants, elected annually by the freemen. Four times a year a general assembly was to be held to make all laws and to admit suitable men to citizenship. This body should also decide what liberties the colonists should enjoy.

Many Englishmen soon left the old country in order to live in this democracy established in the new world, especially when the laws against non-conformists made life in England uncomfortable for most Calvinists. Meanwhile, the king of England ordered the colony to give up its charter, but the company refused to do so without a vote of the assembly. In 1635 the king decided to seize the charter. Troubles at home prevented him from carrying out his threat.

In the Massachusetts Bay colony a typical Calvinistic community was established. Anglicans were shipped back to England. Calvinist ministers were well provided for and a theocracy in which they wielded much power was established. Church membership was a prerequisite for suffrage, while the Bible was the only law book recognized by the church. Inasmuch as the preachers were the best interpreters, they were consulted by magistrates on important questions.

"Blue laws" were rigidly enforced in this colony. No boy under 21, or girl under 18, could be out after nine o'clock without parental permission. A bachelor was regarded with special suspicion and alarm. He, these Calvinists believed, was at best a slacker, and at worst a menace to the morals of the community.

Social life had its pleasant moments. Military drill was a recreation, prizes being given for good marksmanship. Moreover, funerals became social events. So much money was spent on them that laws were passed regulating the cost. The midweek preaching service was almost as attractive as the funerals. It was not uncommon for people to travel from one village to another to attend these meetings.

The settlers in this colony were from all walks of life.

A goodly number of merchants carried on a lucrative fishing and fur trade. In the seventeenth century a glass factory was established at Salem and iron works at Lynn. Most of the settlers, however, were farmers. Nevertheless, business from the first was an important activity in this Puritan settlement. It was not long before the keenness of the New Englander in trade bargains became famous. These Calvinist communities with their strict discipline were able to create a moral, an enterprising, a thrifty, and an independent people, capable of erecting a large part of the foundation upon which rests this nation. To Americans this was the outstanding contribution of Calvinism.

CONCLUSION

Calvinism has been the object of severe criticism by many sincere men. Samuel Butler's description of "The Puritan" in his *Hudibras* (1667-8) will today find many supporters, especially when he wrote:

> A sect whose chief devotion lies
> In odd perverse antipathies;
> In falling out with that or this,
> And finding somewhat still amiss;
> More peevish, cross, and splenetic,
> Than dog distract, or monkey sick:
> That with more care keep holyday
> The wrong, than others the right way;
> Compound for sins they are inclin'd to,
> By damning those they have no mind to:
> Still so perverse and opposite,
> As if they worshipped God for spite:
> The self-same thing they will abhor
> One way, and long another for:
> Freewill they one way disavow,
> Another, nothing else allow:
> All piety consists therein
> In them, in other men sin:

Rather than fail, they will defy
That which they love most tenderly;
Quarrel with minc'd-pies and disparage
Their best and dearest friend, plum-porridge;
Fat pig and goose itself oppose,
And blaspheme custard through the nose.

To see no good in Calvinism is to fail to understand a movement which has done much to shape the activities and ideas of men and women. Most people, it is true, abhor the rigid "blue laws" so strictly enforced by Calvinists in early days. But one must not fail to appreciate the spirit behind those laws—the desire to save souls and to create a kingdom of God on earth. Indeed, most Catholics and Protestants today accept the Calvinistic emphasis upon moral discipline, even though they refuse to adopt the narrow and hard Calvinistic interpretation of this idea.

If Calvinism were purely a moral force, we might leave it to theologians and philosophers. But it was important politically and economically, as well. It was not altogether responsible for democracy, or for the prosperous bourgeois system, nevertheless, it was the theological crystallization of what discontented, fearless men were doing. In giving religious sanction to political resistance and to economic activity it did much to accelerate the forces which made possible our present political and social order. Most important, Calvinism is the backbone of a great part of contemporary Protestantism. As such it was one of the great movements which played an important part in the creation of the modern age.

BIBLIOGRAPHICAL NOTE

Numerous books have been written on the subject of this volume. Many are out of date, or are works designed to prove the validity of some religious doctrine, or are superficial. These, for the most part, have been eliminated. This bibliography lists a few books with which one unfamiliar in the field might well make a beginning.

Of the brief general histories dealing with the religious revolt, Preserved Smith's *The Age of the Reformation* (1920) is outstanding. In it the author discusses the economic, social, moral, intellectual, and political forces of that period. Williston Walker's *The Reformation* (1900) and E. M. Hulme's *The Renaissance, the Protestant Revolution, and the Catholic Reformation in Continental Europe* (1914) are also useful. Of the three books mentioned above, Walker's work contains the best treatment of Calvinism.

Of the general works the most important for the beginner are *The Encyclopædia Britannica* (ed. 14, 24 vols., 1929), containing many excellent articles, *The New International Encyclopædia* (ed. 2, 23 vols., 1930), equally valuable, and the *Realencyklopädie für Protestantische Theologie und Kirche,* edited by J. J. Herzog (24 vols., 1896-1913). The latter is indispensable to the student of church history. Of no less importance is the *Catholic Encyclopædia* (17 vols., 1913-1922). In this excellent work the Catholic view on any religious subject can always be found.

Three great coöperative works contain important

volumes devoted to various aspects of this subject. They are: (1) *The Cambridge Modern History,* planned by Lord Acton, edited by A. W. Ward, G. W. Prothero, Stanley Leathes (14 vols, 1902-1912, see vols. I-III, 1902-1904); (2) *Histoire Générale du IVe siècle à nos jours,* edited by Alfred Rambaud and Ernest Lavisse (12 vols., 1893-1901, see vols. IV-V, 1894-1895); and (3) *Weltgeschichte; hrsg. von J.A.G. von Pflugk-Harttung: Das Religiöse Zeitalter, 1500-1650* (1907-1909). The English and French histories contain lengthy but uncritical bibliographies.

Biographies of John Calvin are numerous. The outstanding brief treatments are: Theodore Béza, *The Life of John Calvin,* translated by Henry Beveridge (1909); L. Penning, *Life and Times of Calvin,* translated from the Dutch by Rev. B. S. Berrington (1912); H. Y. Reyburn, *John Calvin; his Life, Letters and Work* (1914); and Williston Walker, *John Calvin, the Organiser of Reformed Protestantism, 1509-1564* (1906).

The monumental work on Calvin, however, is Émile Doumergue's *Jean Calvin, les hommes et les choses de son temps* (7 vols., 1899-1927).

A number of stimulating interpretations of Calvinism have appeared recently. Among these H. D. Foster's *Collected Papers . . . ; Historical and Biographical Studies* (1929), Quirinus Breen's *John Calvin; a Study in French Humanism* (1931), G. E. Harkness's *John Calvin; the Man and His Ethics* (1931), and B. B. Warfield's *Calvin and Calvinism,* edited by E. D. Warfield (1931), should be mentioned.

Two thoughtful works on Calvin's religious ideas are Paul Lobstein's *Études sur la pensée et l'œuvre de Calvin* (1927) and Alfred de Quervain's *Calvin. Sein Lehren und Kampfen* (1926). In the last book the author emphasizes the international character of Calvin's thinking, devoting one study to Calvin's ideas on liberty and on authority. Allan Menzies, in his volume entitled *A Study of Calvin and Other Papers* (1918), has written an enthusiastic account of Calvin, of his church organization, and of his influence.

A number of suggestive books on the economic significance of Calvinism have appeared recently. Henri Hauser in his *Les débuts du capitalisme* (1927) shows that the justification of commerce by Calvin was not new, but that his sanctification of work was a reaction against medieval ideas. R. H. Tawney, in his *Religion and the Rise of Capitalism* (1926) describes exceedingly well the Puritan exaltation of middle-class virtues. G. A. T. O'Brien's, *An Essay on the Economic Effects of the Reformation* (1923), Werner Sombart's *Der Moderne Kapitalismus* (3 vols. in 6, 1928), and Max Weber's *The Protestant Ethic and the Spirit of Capitalism,* translated by Talcott Parsons (1930), also contain excellent interpretations of the economic importance of Calvinism.

No student of this subject should fail to read some of the works of John Calvin, especially his *Institutes.* There are numerous translations of Calvin's *Institutes.* Of these, *The Institutes of the Christian Religion,* translated by John Allen (Amer. ed. 6. rev. and corr., 2 vols., 1928) is probably the best. *The Letters of John Calvin,* compiled by Jules Bonnet, translated from the original Latin and French by David Constable (2 vols., 1855-1857), throw much light on this interesting personality.

For additional information on the subject, Calvinism and the French civil wars, one should consult Edward Armstrong's *The French Wars of Religion; their Political Aspects* (1892), Louis Batiffol's *The Century of the Renaissance,* translated from the French by E. F. Buckley with an introduction by J. E. C. Bodley (1916),

F. C. Palm's *Politics and Religion in Sixteenth-Century France* (1927), A. A. Tilley's *The French Wars of Religion* (1919), and J. W. Thompson's *The Wars of Religion in France, 1559-76* (1909). These books bring out the importance of Calvinism in France. The standard work in French on this period is the *Histoire de France,* edited by Ernest Lavisse (9 vols., 1904-1911). H. M. Baird's, *History of the Rise of the Huguenots of France* (2 vols., 1879) and *The Huguenots and Henry of Navarre* (2 vols., 1886), while out of date, are still the best Protestant accounts of the Huguenots to be found in the English language.

Books dealing with special phases of the religious wars are noteworthy. Of these Joseph de Croze's, *Les Guises, Les Valois, et Philippe II* (2 vols., 1866), Francis De Crue de Stoutz's *Le parti des politiques au lendemain de la Saint-Barthélemy. La Molle et Coconat* (1892), Félix Rocquain's *La France et Rome pendant les guerres de religion* (1924), G. J. Weill's *Les théories sur le pouvoir royal en France pendant les guerres de religion* (1892), John Vienot's *Histoire de la réforme française des origines à l'édit de Nantes* (1926), contain scholarly accounts of the political aspects of the religious wars. F. C. Palm's *The Establishment of French Absolutism (1574-1610)* in *Landmarks in History* series (1928) contains translations of published and unpublished documents dealing with the French religious wars.

For Calvinism in Italy and in central Europe, the following general works are valuable: F. C. Church's *The Italian Reformers, 1534-1564* (1932); Charles Beard, *Martin Luther and the Reformation in Germany Until the Close of the Diet of Worms* (1889); T. M. Lindsay, *A History of the Reformation* (2 vols., 1913-1914); Leopold von Ranke, *History of the Reformation in Germany,* translated by Sarah Austin, edited by R. A. Johnson (1905); Philip Schaff, *History of the Christian Church* (7 vols., in 8, 1882-1910); and H. C. Vedder, *The Reformation in Germany* (1914). For special accounts read Paul Fox's *The Reformation in Poland, some social and economic aspects* (1924); [Jessie Bedford's] *Heidelberg* [Elizabeth Godfrey, pseud.] (1906); and Frank Puaux's *Histoire de l'establissement des Protestants Français en Suède* (1891).

For Calvinism in Holland, P. J. Blok's *History of the People of the Netherlands,* translated by Ruth Putnam and O. A. Bierstadt (5 vols., 1898-1912), J. L. Motley's *History of the United Netherlands* (6 vols., 1900), and *The Rise of the Dutch Republic, a History* (3 vols., 1909), should be consulted. In addition to these standard works, J. E. Barker's *The Rise and Decline of the Netherlands* (1906); Edward Armstrong's *The Emperor Charles V* (2 vols., 1902); D. B. Wyndham Lewis's *Charles of Europe* (1931); R. B. Merriman's *The Rise of the Spanish Empire in the Old World and the New* (3 vols., 1918-1925); Ludwig Häusser's *The Period of the Reformation, 1517-1648,* translated by Mrs. George Sturge (1873); Ruth Putnam's *William the Silent* (1911); and J. L. Motley's *The Life and Death of John of Barneveld, Advocate of Holland* (2 vols., 1904) are useful.

For Calvinism in Scotland the general histories of the reformation should be consulted. P. H. Brown's *History of Scotland* (3 vols., 1909-1912); and Andrew Lang's *A History of Scotland from the Roman Occupation* (4 vols., 1900-1907) also contain important information on this subject. In addition, of the biographies of John Knox, P. H. Brown's *John Knox, a Biography* (2 vols., 1895), Henry Cowan's *John Knox, the Hero of the Scottish Reformations* (1905), Andrew Lang's *John Knox and the Reformation* (1905), and Edwin Muir's *John*

Knox, Portrait of a Calvinist (1929), are worth reading. For an excellent bibliographical guide consult A. R. Anderson's *A Short Bibliography on Scottish History and Literature* (1922). *The Works of John Knox,* edited by David Laing (6 vols., 1846-1864) and John Knox, *The History of the Reformation of Religion in Scotland,* edited by Cuthbert Lennox (1905), throw light on one of the outstanding followers of Calvin.

For Calvinism in England the following volumes from *The Political History of England,* edited by William Hunt and R. L. Poole, are valuable: H. A. L. Fisher's *The History of England from the Accession of Henry VII to the Death of Henry VIII, 1485-1547* (new edition, 1913), vol. V; A. F. Pollard's *The History of England from the Accession of Edward I to the Death of Elizabeth, 1547-1603* (1910), vol. VI. G. M. Trevelyan's *England Under the Stuarts* (1925) should also be consulted. In addition to these works, Henry Gee's *The Reformation Period* in *Handbooks of English Church History,* IV (1909), Frederic Harrison's *Oliver Cromwell* (1888) and T. B. M. Macaulay's *Milton* (1900) are suggestive. J. A. Froude's *History of England from the Fall of Wolsey to the Death of Elizabeth* (12 vols., 1856-1870) is still one of the best accounts available, although it is strongly royalist and Protestant. H. L. Clarke's *Studies in the English Reformation* (1912) should be read. For other special works on this subject consult the bibliographies in *The Cambridge Modern History* and *The Political History of England* by William Hunt and R. L. Poole. Interesting documents relating to Calvinism may be found in *Documents Illustrative of English Church History,* compiled by Henry Gee and by W. J. Hardy (1896), *Select Statutes and Other Constitutional Documents Illustrative of the Reigns of Elizabeth and*

James I, edited by G. W. Prothero (ed. 4. 1913) and S. R. Gardiner's *The Constitutional Documents of the Puritan Revolution, 1625-1660* (ed. 3. 1906).

For Calvinism in the Americas the following works will be found useful: C. W. Baird, *History of the Huguenot Immigration to America* (2 vols., 1885), E. H. Byington, *The Puritan as a Colonist and Reformer* (1899), J. A. Goodwin, *The Pilgrim Republic* (1888), T. C. Hall, *The Religious Background of an American Culture* (1930), H. W. Lawrence, *The Not-quite Puritans* (1928), S. E. Morison, *Builders of the Bay Colony* (1930), H. W. Schneider, *The Puritan Mind* (1930), L. G. Tyler, *England in America, 1580-1652,* in *American Nation* series, vol. IV (1904), and R. G. Usher, *The Pilgrims and Their History* (1918). An interesting contemporary account of this subject may be found in William Bradford's *History of the Plymouth Settlement, 1608-1650,* rendered into modern English by Valerian Paget (1909). For additional works consult Edward Channing, A. B. Hart, and F. J. Turner, *Guide to the Study and Reading of American History* (rev. and augm. ed. 1912).

INDEX

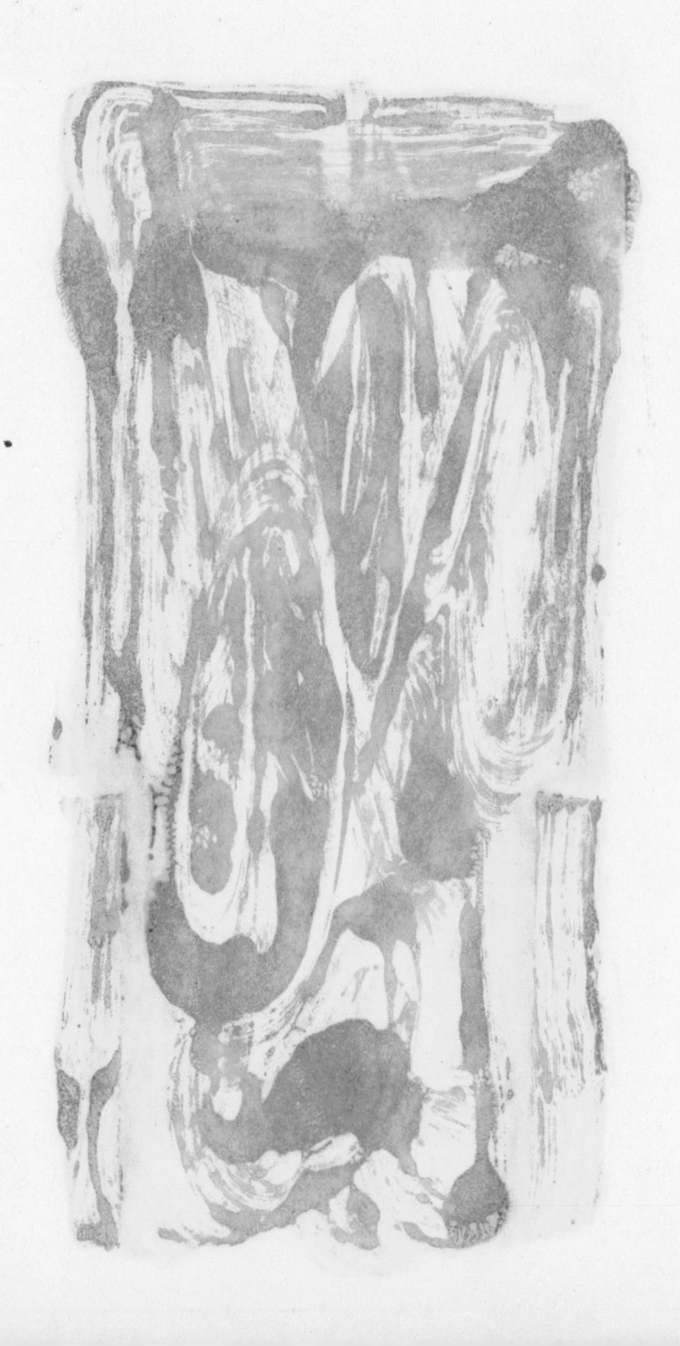